Will Jones' Space Adventures & The Zadrilian Queen (The Space Masters)©

Christine Thompson-Wells

Other books in this series:

Will Jones' Space Adventures and the Money Formula

Out soon:

Will Jones' Space Adventures
& The Children of the Black Sun

Will Jones' Space Adventures & The Zadrilian Queen (The Space Masters) ©

Christine Thompson-Wells

Drawings: Brian Platt

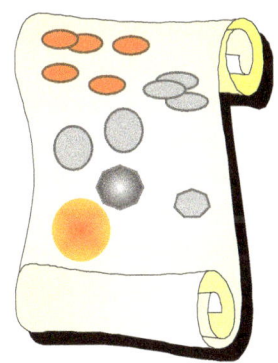

If you have purchased this book without its cover, it may be a stolen book. This should be reported to the publisher.

This publication is written and is intended to provide reliable and competent information. Neither the publisher nor the author is under any obligation to provide professional services in rendering financial and legal advice or otherwise.

The law and practices vary from country to country and state to state. If legal or professional information is required, the purchaser or the reader should seek the information privately and best suited to their particular circumstances.

The author and the publisher specifically disclaim any liability that may be incurred from the information within this book.

All rights reserved. No part of this book, including the interior design, cover design and icons may be reproduced or transmitted in any form by any means (electronic, photocopying, recording or otherwise) without the prior permission of the publisher.

ISBN: 978–0–9551498–3–2

Copyright © 2002, 2008 reprint, 2017, 2020
by Christine Thompson-Wells
All rights reserved.
Published by Books For Reading On Line. Com for MSI International
see our web site: www.booksforreadingonline.com
Email: sales@booksforreadingonline.com

Edited and laid out by John Firth

Contents   Page

Chapter One   1
A Visit from the Grigan Leader
Chapter Two   12
The Green Light
Chapter Three   20
The Space Master Ziob
Chapter Four   32
Will Meets the Lizard People from the Planet Zadril
Chapter Five   42
A Hazardous Voyage
Chapter Six   56
Will Learns More about the Planet and the People of Zadril
Chapter Seven   68
Princess Eex and the Butler Meet a Messenger
Chapter Eight   85
The Planetary Storm, and After
Chapter Nine   93
The Green Light and Princess Eex
Chapter Ten   110
The Giant in the Mountain Pass
Chapter Eleven   118
Princess Eex Learns More
Chapter Twelve   134
What a Surprise!
Chapter Thirteen   146
The Journey to Ozimoth

With love to Emma, Ashley & Felicia

Foreword

Will Jones works for a farmer on the island of Ozimoth, on Planet Earth. He had worked very hard over the last two weeks. He was on his way home and had just been paid his wages by the farmer.

Will was thinking about everything as he rode his bike along the sandy, rock-and-gravel road. He clearly was not concentrating on what he should have been doing – riding his bike safely!

In a flash his bike wheel ran into a rock and Will was thrown off the bike and onto the hard gravelly edge at the side of the road next to a newly ploughed field.

For a short time Will must have lost consciousness. When he awoke he thought he could hear the familiar sound of something he knew well, but he wasn't sure! He thought silently, 'Am I really hearing the sound or is it something I'm imagining?

He was soon to find out that his mind was not playing tricks and Yes, he was now to go on another space adventure: to the Planet Grigan and beyond!

Chapter One

A Visit From The Grigan Leader

Will had worked very hard for the farmer during a hot summer's day. It was evening and still hot by the time he had finished working for the day.

'One good thing about today,' thought Will. 'It's payday!' Will was feeling very good about how much money he had earned over the last two weeks.

Because Will had also worked very hard, when the farmer paid him, he told Will, 'I'm giving you some extra money this payday; it's a bonus and "thank you" for all the extra work you have done this last fortnight.' The farmer continued, 'You have a ten per cent bonus in your pay this fortnight, Will.'

Will knew he earned five rupins an hour, and he had worked four hours yesterday, Saturday, and two hours today, Sunday. He now started to work out, in his head, how much money he had been paid altogether. He thought to himself, 'The farmer doesn't often pay the people who work for him extra money, and he is "known to be rather mean" !'

The fact that Will was paid extra left him very surprised indeed. He thought, as he rode his bike home, '...that is so unusual; the farmer has never given me extra money before!'

Will was trying to work out his money while riding his bike – his first mistake! He was thinking very deeply, and had put the pay envelope containing the money into his jeans' pocket, deciding, '…I will work it out later when I get home.' As he rode, he wasn't thinking very clearly; there were so many things going through his head, all at once. He thought, 'I've arranged to meet Ben later this evening and now it's getting really late!'

He cycled too fast; he was going over lumpy, stony, sandy ground; suddenly he felt the wheels of his bike move sideways and he felt his body being thrown from the bike, into the air and then down hard onto the ground.

Will lay on the ground unable to move for a few minutes. His head was hurting, and he couldn't think straight! He was lying on the grass at the side of the road and continued looking up into the sky.

He thought he heard a familiar sound: '…the sound of what?' he asked himself. As the fuzziness cleared from his mind, he thought 'Is that the sound, the sound?' Again he listened! He knew, he knew the sound; there it was again and again, he thought.

He now felt his body; his legs and arms; he wiggled his toes and fingers; he realised, 'I can still move them!'

Will was starting to recover from the fall and decided to jump up. He did this, but as he did so, his head hurt. He could now see stars in the sky, '…or were they?' he wondered. He waited again for his head to clear; he slowly started to feel better; he then heard the sound again, coming from high up in the sky!

'I know that sound...' he thought again. 'It's the sound of a spaceship's engine!' he said out loud. Realising he had done this, he felt foolish and was very glad that nobody was around to hear him.

Will heard the sound of 'whirring and whirring' engines again and then once more. He was now sure and shouted out, 'It's a spaceship, a spaceship!' This time, he didn't care who heard him!

He looked around and couldn't see any signs of a spaceship or anything that resembled a spaceship! He was trying to think through the situation but his thinking was in a muddle; he said to himself, 'I do feel very muddle-headed at the moment and cannot really think clearly...' He waited and then listened again, much more carefully this time. He thought, 'I will wait to hear the sound again!' He waited, then, he could hear the sound of the spaceship's engines. Clearly this time, he heard the familiar sound!

He waited patiently for something to happen.

Will still felt shaky from his fall and decided to sit back down on the grass. The sun was setting; he had thought he had seen stars in the sky. But now, as he collected his thoughts, he realised that maybe it had been the reflection of the sun on the spaceship's surface. He wanted to be sure. 'I'll wait here and listen and watch for a spaceship,' then, 'If I don't see or hear a spaceship again, I will wait until I feel better, then I will try to get home!'

The puzzled boy let some time pass and waited to hear or see if there was a spaceship close by. At last, when he didn't hear or see anything, he decided, he might as well walk home with his bike.

Up to this point he hadn't stopped to look at the condition of his bike. He sat thinking for a while and then stood up again.

He hadn't given his bike another thought until, lifting it out of the long grass, he could see how much damage had been done to the front wheel in the accident. 'It's buckled,' he knew instantly, and thought, 'I will have to walk all the way home and carry or drag my bike in the best way that I can!'

This new problem made him forget about the sound of the spaceship's engines. Will started the long walk home and as he did so, he thought, 'I know I will be late to meet Ben, but I can't do much about it!'

He had left his mobile phone at home that morning; he knew now the only thing to do was walk and get home as quickly as possible. He realised, as he pushed and pulled the broken bike over tufts of grass, 'that it's going to be hard work to get home in time… to say the least!'

He was thinking about the day's work he had finished and felt good that he had worked so hard for the farmer. He also touched the money he had earned, and Yes, that was still in his jeans' pocket. As he felt the packet of money, he could feel the shape of the coins in the envelope. He was deeply in thought as he continued his journey home along the dirt road close to the field and the sea.

Whirring, whirring sounds could be heard again, over his head; he looked up and there from the window of the spaceship he saw the Great Grigan Leader waving to him. Will was astonished, and thought, 'Is that the Leader, here on Ozimoth, from the Planet Grigan? If it is the Great Grigan Leader,' he thought, 'I can't believe I'm really seeing him!'

He waved back and shouted to him, 'Great Leader, why are you here?' The Grigan Leader's spaceship slowly landed in the field next to where Will had been walking with his broken bike.

As the ship zoomed to a stop after whirling around and around on the ploughed earth of the field, the Grigan Leader and a Griganian Elder came out from behind a sliding, shining silver door in the ship. The two space people walked briskly towards Will and were soon right in front of him!

At first they spoke in their native tongue, but started to realise that Will did not understand what they were saying. Very slowly, both Will and the visitors began to speak in a way that they all understood!

'The Elder is as fearsome-looking as the Grigan Leader without his battle helmet on!' thought Will.

The Grigan Leader looked at Will and said, 'My young friend, be careful what you think!' Will knew the rules of thinking on other planets: 'if you want to think about people only think nice things!' He felt embarrassed at forgetting such a simple rule.

No sooner had the Grigan Leader told Will to think in the way of the planets than, beaming, he scooped Will up into his arms and said, 'It's very good to see you, young friend. We watched you take a tumble on your bike, but we could do nothing about it. Are you hurt?'

Will said in a reassuring voice, 'No, Great Leader, I'm fine, thank you; as you can see, I'm a lot better off than my bike!' He looked down at his very broken bike wheel and knew that all of his special money was going to be needed to put the bike into riding order again. Will also knew his mum and dad would not let him ride it again until it was completely fit to ride on the road!

The Grigan Leader looked at Will and said, 'Aren't you supposed to be wearing a safety helmet?' Will knew this was a number one rule at home and he was also going to get into serious trouble for not wearing his helmet.

The Grigan Leader knew he had said enough about the helmet and decided to let Will's dad take on the next part of the telling-off!

Will looked at the ground, feeling he had let his mum and dad down by breaking such a vital rule. He knew he was going to get into serious trouble… and he was supposed to meet Ben later! All of these thoughts were going around in his head. 'Yet,' he thought, 'I'm so very glad to see the Grigan Leader standing before me, in a field in Ozimoth!' He knew too, that he was running out of time to do everything he had planned to do that evening.

The Grigan Leader spoke again. 'Will, we need you to help us on the Planet Grigan.' Will had known the Grigan Leader for a long time and was very fond of him, 'but,' he thought, 'Planet Grigan is even further away from Ozimoth than the Planet Spectron!'

The Grigan Leader read Will's thoughts and said, 'We can be on Grigan in a flash, Will!'

Will did not need to think any more about this opportunity and said in reply, 'I would like to see the Planet Grigan.' He continued, 'Before we go, I need to ask, why do you need my help?'

The Grigan Leader replied, 'We would like you to speak to the Intergalactic Space Masters from the Council of Space Elders; the Masters are meeting on Grigan very shortly. We would also like you to talk to our children.'

Will thought again, 'I've never heard of the Space Masters.'

Of course, the Grigan Leader read Will's thoughts and replied, 'I know you have not heard of the Intergalactic Space Masters; they are second in importance only to the Council of Space Elders and are very wise, but they too need to learn new ways and new things.' He continued, 'they are also very interested in the way you work with your money, Will.'

Will carefully thought about what the Grigan Leader had just said, then looked at his bike and asked, 'Where shall I leave my bike?'

The Grigan Leader knew before Will had asked the question. He replied, 'We will take it to Grigan. I'm sure the children of Grigan would like to see a bike like that, Will!'

Will thought for a bit before allowing his mind to really run away. He then thought, 'I don't think my bike is so different!'

The Grigan Leader looked at Will and replied, 'Oh, yes, Will, our bikes are very different to the bikes on Ozimoth!' The Grigan Leader chuckled as he made this last remark!

Will didn't know if the Grigan Leader was being smart, or if he really meant his remark in a nice way!

Before he could blink, Griganian space soldiers were out of the spaceship and lifting Will's bike into it. Will then followed the group into the ship, ready for the journey to the Planet Grigan.

Whirring, whirring, whirring, the engines of the ship started; it rose into the sky and then sped out into space. 'Now it is in outer space and a very long way from Ozimoth!' thought Will.

The ship was travelling fast, at 'hyper-sonic' speed, it seemed to him. He could not remember ever being in a spaceship that had moved at this speed.

As Will looked out of the spaceship's window they passed the Planet of Spectron; now he could see the Planet of Majania and the Planet of The Black Sun in the distance! Looking at the Planet of the Black Sun, for some reason, sent a chill down his spine! He shuddered as he continued to stare at the enormous planet. The Grigan Leader, seeing what he was looking at, told him, 'That is a bad place, Will. It is always dark there. It is dangerous to go to the Planet of the Black Sun.'

Will looked at his watch. He had fallen off his bike at about five-fifteen; his watch-hands now showed it was 'five-seventeen.' He looked again at his watch a little time later: 'it is still at five-seventeen!' he thought silently.

The Grigan Leader looked at Will and Will could see into the slot of the Leader's helmet. He was sure, he thought, that he saw one of the Leader's very large eyes wink back at him!

The Grigan Leader then said, 'Will, look ahead; it's Grigan. Look, right ahead!' he said again.

Will looked and could see the massive Planet Grigan. 'It's much larger than the Planet of Spectron!' he realised. As the spaceship travelled closer to the large, circling planet, Will saw blue- and green rings spiralling round and round it!

Will said to the Grigan Leader, 'It's beautiful: I had no idea the Planet Grigan would look like this.' As Will made these comments, the Grigan Leader stood very upright and his chest became larger and larger, filling his Leader's uniform to the maximum! Will, looking at him, thought 'His chest will soon explode if it expands any more!' The Grigan Leader was so preoccupied with looking at his planet he had missed Will's last thoughts! Will, seeing how proud the Leader was of his planet and home, realised how much the Leader had wanted him to see it.

Will also felt very proud to know a man like the Grigan Leader.

Chapter Two

The Green Light

The ship was now closer to the planet and Will couldn't help but look at his watch again; it was now almost five-seventeen and thirty seconds. 'There are still more seconds to go before the second hand will pass thirty!' he thought. He realised, 'we only left Ozimoth two-and-a-half minutes ago!' Shaking his head in disbelief, he thought how impossible it all seemed.

The spaceship was now very close to Grigan and coming in to land. Will could make out buildings and see people walking in the streets! As quickly as they had taken off, they put down at what looked liked a landing strip in the middle of a large green field. Green grass was everywhere: 'as far as the eye could see!' Will realised. The Grigan Leader came over and stood with Will. Will continued gazing out of the spaceship's windows at the green and blue planet.

The Leader said, 'Once upon a time, during the great wars, this land was just sand and dried soil. We have worked with the King of Spectron and his people and now you can see how good the land is. The King and the people of Spectron have told us many secrets about how to care and work with our planet.'

He continued to speak to Will, his voice full of pride: 'Of course, there are some parts of the planet that we still need to care for but, by the time it has once more circled round the suns, the whole of the Planet Grigan will look like this.'

The door of the spaceship was now sliding sideways, and the soldiers waited patiently for their Leader to leave it. The Grigan Leader walked out first, followed by the Griganian Elder and then Will. After these three, a Griganian soldier had picked up and was carrying Will's broken bike. 'He must be as strong as an ox. The soldier picked up my bike like it was a matchstick!' thought Will. The soldier looked towards Will and the boy thought he could see a faint glimmer in the Griganian soldier's deep black eyes, as if he knew Will's thoughts!

Will asked the soldier, 'What are you going to do with my bike?' The soldier didn't reply. The Grigan Leader turned to Will instead and said, 'We will fix it!'

Will was now very quiet as they all walked towards the great green and blue buildings of the great city of Jade. His breath was taken away by what he saw and what he was experiencing on this planet! In the middle of the city there was a building larger than any Will had ever seen. 'None of the planets I've visited have a building this big!' he thought.

The Grigan Leader looked at Will again and Will thought he saw a wink come from the deep blackness of the

Grigan Leader's eyes. Then suddenly, a faint smile appeared on the lumpy, bumpy lips in the lumpy, bumpy face of the Leader.

The blue and green building was shining and splendid in the glare of the Griganian suns, Will noticed. They continued walking towards it, through streets of shining green stone and shining green houses. Will stopped to speak to some children who were playing hop and cross on the pathway. Will knew this game, as both he and Ben had played it with the children of Spectron.

The Grigan Leader's party stopped too; they also spoke to the children. After their brief talk, the party continued their walk to the very large blue and green building in the middle of the city. As they came closer it appeared larger than ever before, thought Will. The party entered and passed through some very large gates into a wide park. The soldiers of the party had stopped walking and stood at the gates.

The soldier carrying Will's bike now disappeared in another direction. Will thought, 'He continues to carry the bike like it's a feather.'

Will followed the Grigan Leader and the Griganian Elder. They walked on shiny green pathways and through avenues of very tall green trees, all of the time getting closer to the very large, grand, blue and green building. Then the Grigan Leader stopped and spoke to the Griganian Elder, who left them and walked off in another direction. The Leader now said to Will, 'You will now meet the Royal Family of Grigan.'

Will was very surprised to hear this and said, 'I thought you were the ruler of the Planet Grigan?'

The Leader smiled and chuckled at Will's comment; he looked at Will and replied, 'I rule and protect the planet and the people of Grigan, but I'm not a member of the Royal Family!'

They now entered the very large blue and green building. They walked through many grand and large green rooms; all of the time, Will could hear children laughing and playing. Suddenly, they found themselves in a very large green room: the walls appeared to be of green glass, the floors too looked like green glass, or a stone like malachite. As Will looked up, high above in the ceiling he saw a green glass chandelier. So large was the chandelier that it seemed to Will to take up the whole ceiling.

He looked around. 'I've never seen anything so grand,' he thought. The Leader looked at him and nodded his head. Will felt he wanted to touch the green walls and floor but knew, 'I will have to wait to do that. Wait for something?' he thought. He didn't know what, but he just knew, somehow, he had to wait!

The great green doors to yet another green room suddenly opened and a king in rich green robes, with a queen in a fine rich green gown, walked into the room.

So did one, two, three, four, five, six and then a seventh little child, all dressed in rich green clothes, following their parents. Will observed that the seven children were all different ages and they ran 'hither' and 'thither' throughout the 'very posh rooms of the palace'.

While the children were running around and making a noise, the King and Queen tried to welcome Will to the Planet Grigan. The noisy children laughed and played the whole time the King and Queen were trying to talk!

The King eventually called to them to be silent: 'We have a visitor from the island of Ozimoth,' he said.

The children were curious; they had not seen a person from another planet before. They gathered around Will and started to touch him. By this time the King and Queen were sitting on their high thrones, and they called the children to them. The Leader looked on as the children obeyed their parents. They sat, for a short time, on the high steps that led to the thrones.

When Will looked at the children, he saw four boys and three girls. They were trying to be good in the throne room, but it was very difficult for them to sit still. One boy poked his sister in the stomach and made her giggle.

The Queen was trying to make the children behave; she then called a name and many women, dressed in fine green gowns, came into the throne room to help her look after the children. Slowly, the women in green took the children out of the room. The children all filed past Will and as they did so, touched him on the hand, the knees, his arms and then the oldest boy poked him too, in the stomach. Will looked at the boy and squinted his eyes back at him. Will didn't say anything but somehow knew he would get his own back!

The King and Queen were eager to talk and wanted to learn everything they could about Ozimoth. Will was called up to the thrones and a Griganian Elder, also dressed in a green tunic with a cape of rich green fabric, brought a stool for him to sit on. Will did not know this, but a long conversation was about to begin and it would be mainly about the island of Ozimoth!

Will could not tell the King and Queen enough; they just wanted more and more and more information. They wanted to know about the people; the land, the sun, seas and oceans; the birds, fishes in the seas, flowers, insects, animals; his mother's cooking, what sort of work his father did and how much money he was paid for working. They wanted every piece of information that Will could tell them.

Both suns had long ago set and the moons were now up and Will, the King and Queen of Grigan were still talking. Suddenly, Will felt his head start to roll around and droop from side to side on his shoulders and, before he knew it, he was on the floor next to the thrones sound asleep. The Queen was very worried about this; she ordered him to be taken to a bed at once, to rest!

A large Griganian lifted Will up into his arms. He lifted Will so quickly and easily, it was as though the boy was as light as the wing of a butterfly. He took Will into a bedroom next to the bedrooms of the Royal children.

Needless to say, Will didn't get much rest! Once the children knew Will was in the room next to theirs, they listened at the door and waited for the orderly to leave Will tucked up in bed. Then, as soon as he had disappeared, they ran into Will's room to rouse him. Will, waking up, was startled and, at first, didn't realise what had happened. He looked and saw seven little Griganian faces looking back at him!

Suddenly the noisy children fell very silent. A brilliant green light filled the room. The children stood still without moving an eyelid or a limb. Brighter and brighter the room became. Brilliant green light came flooding into every corner; every nook and, by this time, every part of the room became filled with bright iridescent green rays of light. The children's faces turned greener and greener. Will looked at his arms and they too were turning greener, he realised.

He looked at the children: 'They have not moved a muscle of their bodies,' he thought. He then muttered to himself, not knowing his voice could be heard, 'What could this be; what could make these children suddenly stop everything they were doing?'

The children and Will were now greener and greener, and they were all in a very green room!

Chapter Three

The Space Master Ziob

The children and Will were still standing in the bedroom when the King of Grigan came running in. He asked, in Griganian, 'Are you all alright?' Will looked at the King and then at the children; they all were now returning to their natural colour. Griganian children normally have greenish skin but, while the green rays had played over them, their skin had gone very green indeed, thought Will.

Will also slowly felt his own body return to normal. He suddenly realised he had felt very strange while in the green rays.

Just as this was happening, the Grigan Leader came into the bedroom. He looked around and saw that the King's children were all starting to play again. He looked at Will and scanned him all over, then said, 'How do you feel now, Will?' Will replied, 'Fine.'

The Leader was concerned about the green rays, Will noticed. The King and the Leader now walked out of the room, leaving Will and the seven children behind. Will hadn't thought this was such a good idea. Being left with seven overly energetic children in the middle of the night was not his idea of having a good time! He moved over to the doorway and could see the King and the Leader in deep discussion. They both looked at Will and the King summoned him to come and speak with them.

As Will moved over to join the King and the Leader, he knew by instinct that fourteen eyes were now watching him as he walked across the hall. He turned to look back and the eyes disappeared. He started walking again and felt the eyes watching him once more. He knew they were the eyes of the seven children and this time, he thought, 'I'm not going to look back'.

The children watched while the King of Grigan spoke to Will. The Leader stood rigid and listened to the King speak. He said, 'Will, we need to teach our children some principles of how to work with money, not just our money but the money of other planets. The children need to know how to spend money wisely. Our children need to understand the value of money and what they can buy of value. They need to understand the difference between earned money and gift money.

'Some of our citizens were injured in the wars and our children need to understand how these people are now supported by the other citizens of Grigan.'

The King stroked his greenish beard and took a big breath, then gave a sigh and said, 'And there is so much more for them to learn…!' He moved his crown to one side of his sleek head with his long fingers and scratched his head in disbelief at everything the children of Grigan now needed to learn! He said in desperation, 'It's not just money, but advancing technology too, they need to learn about!' and again he sighed, still scratching his head!

Will wanted to ask what was the thick, green light and why did it come over the Planet Grigan as it had? The Grigan Leader was using telepathy and knew exactly what Will was going to ask. He said to the King, 'Your Majesty, I must take Will to the Building of Knowledge where he can meet some Learned Ones, and they will help him to understand your wishes.'

The Leader bent his lumpy, bumpy head forward towards the King, slowly turned and walked away. Will then, humbly, followed the Grigan Leader.

As they were walking to the Building of Knowledge, thick green rays of light swept over the planet again. The eerie green light was searching between the many moonbeams on the planet. This time the light was much greener and thicker, 'and becoming thicker by the space second!' Will noticed.

The Leader pushed Will behind a very large tree. He spoke in Griganian, which Will strangely seemed now to understand, saying, 'Don't move, stay there, I will be back in a short moon time.' Will knew he had to do as the Leader had asked.

He waited and waited for the Grigan Leader to return. He waited 'even longer' he thought, 'than I expected to have to wait!' He waited for so long that he decided to make himself comfortable and sat down under the tree in the middle of the City of Jade while the green light grew thicker and thicker.

Will could now feel the green rays of light; he could now touch the light and noticed it had a type of smell. He thought, 'I know that smell!' He thought again to himself, 'what is that smell?' He continued thinking and asking himself what the smell was. He continued analysing the smell and started to answer his own questions. 'It smells a bit like the swamps around Ozimoth, but somehow different!' he thought. He thought for a while longer and knew he recognised the smell, but just couldn't think of where he had smelled it before.

He was thinking very deeply about the thick green light and its powerful rays, when the ground, where he was sitting, started to move. The Grigan Leader had not returned and Will was now feeling a little worried. He knew he had to stay by the big tree and just wait. But the ground under him moved again and again.

As the ground moved it suddenly started to break open into a hole, which grew larger and deeper. Will felt his body move towards the hole. He tried to grab the branches of the tree so that he would not fall into what now appeared a very large hole in the ground of the Planet Grigan. It was too late; the branches moved further and further from his grasp as he started to fall down the large and ever-growing hole. He then tried to grab the huge tree roots but soon he had fallen past them, falling, falling, deeper and deeper into the very large hole in the ground!

The thick green light rays too were following him down the hole. The light was moving as quickly as he was. Down and down they fell together; side by side they tumbled deeper and deeper into the hole.

The distance was so vast that Will had time to wonder when he would reach the bottom of the hole. Both the thick green rays and Will were travelling together, at greater and greater speed.

Will could feel his hair almost lifting from his head. His shirt too! With the speed, his shirt kept being pulled up over his head and at times he couldn't see where he was going as he fell faster and faster!

Suddenly, the thick green light rays and Will started to slow down. Slower and slower they both fell. They were now falling so slowly that they were almost standing together as they travelled through the space in the hole under the large green tree. Soon the bottom of the hole was in sight. Will could make out many other green shapes as his feet suddenly found a landing spot. The thick green light had also reached the same landing spot, its rays now dancing and spiralling around in the empty space.

Will started to straighten his clothes. His shirt had almost left his body. He had been travelling at such a great speed, down and down into the deep, deep hole, that his fingers and toes were numb! During this time, Will was not aware of the shape that the thick green light was adopting. Busily adjusting to his new surroundings, Will suddenly turned to see the distinctive green shape of a space being emerging!

He strained his eyes to see if he could see more of the thick green light and the being. He thought for a moment and asked himself, 'Where will I hide; where will I run to; how can I escape from this?'

He looked around and all he could see was the blackness of the hole and many strange green glowing shapes appearing! He thought, 'I could not hide or run even if I wanted to.' He decided, 'I have no choice; I will have to stand and wait for the shape to appear completely and see what happens then.'

Now, standing there before him, Will could see a person in glowing green robes, wearing a green crown and holding a shining green sword in her hand. She had long flowing purple hair and brilliant pink eyes. The green being looked at Will through her pink eyes and Will felt the power of her stare.

He waited and then decided to speak. 'Hello, I'm Will Jones and I live on the island of Ozimoth. Who are you?'

The green person then spoke in a language Will had not heard before, but strangely he understood what the figure was saying. She said, 'I'm Ziob, a Space Master.'

Will then quickly answered, 'I'm very glad to make your acquaintance.' Will felt very assertive and continued, 'May I ask, why are we down in this hole in the ground together?'

Ziob was clearly a little taken aback by Will's abruptness and questions and, after taking a little time, said 'We are here to work together. We are here to prepare the children for their next lessons in learning.'

Will listened with interest to Ziob's words. Slowly she turned and lifted her sword into the black air of Grigan's deep inner space. A gentle green light began to glow from the sword and the black space became lighter, then brighter and brighter than anything Will had ever seen. He was now seeing a brilliant green-lit area deep within the central core of Grigan's planet.

More green shapes started to emerge, growing larger within this vast deep space under the ground.

There were triangles, pentagons, hexagons, heptagons, octagons, squares, parallelograms, rectangles, rhombi, circles, cubes and trapezia all there before Will.

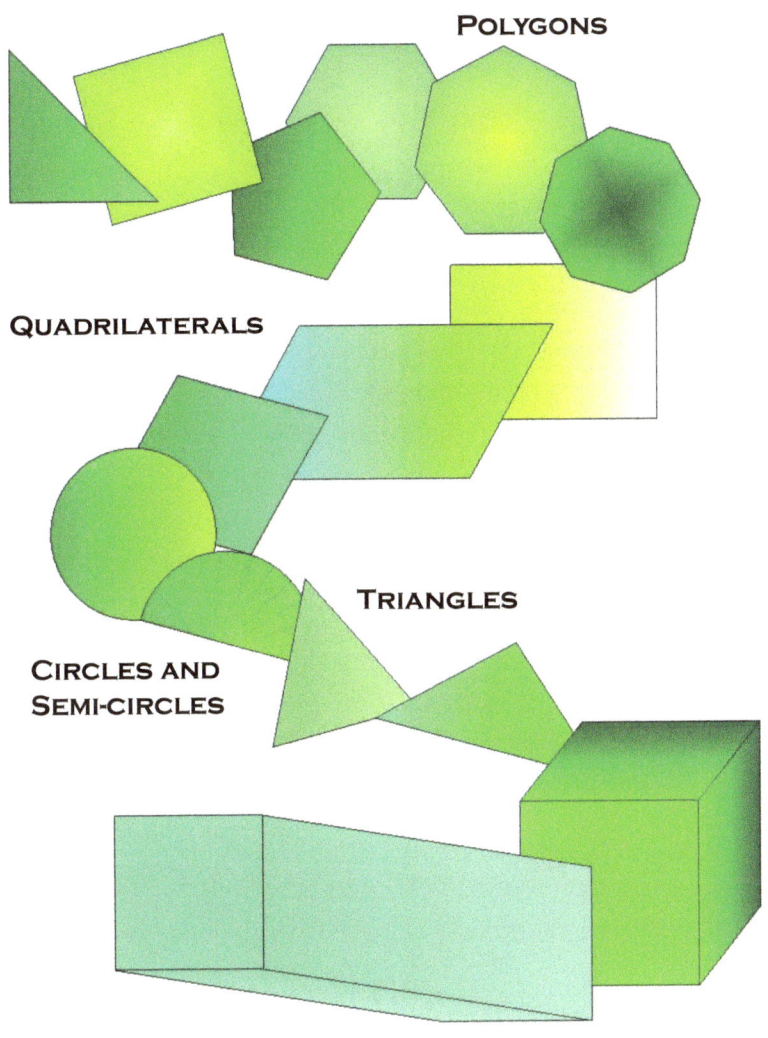

Ziob then said, 'You are now within the City of Epahs, which exists deep within the Planet of Grigan. I work with other Space Masters, but I am the only one that lives at Epahs.' She took a breath. 'The Space Masters study the way that people think. The Space Masters know that thinking now is different to what it was many generations ago. We need to think of new ways and to help people think of new ways about their problems during this moons' and suns' time.'

Ziob continued, 'We also know that the people of the planet want to trade with other planets and, to do this, they need to be educated in commerce and trade. To become so they will need to change the way they think about buying and selling, growing crops and farming animals.'

Will found what the Space Master had to say very interesting. He thought suddenly about his Grandma on Ozimoth and said to Ziob, 'I have heard my Grandma say "Oh we used to think differently in our day" !' Even Ziob, a serious and stern Space Master, had to smile at Will's comment.

Will also knew that. He thought, 'Ozimoth is now taking part in intergalactic trade and has been doing so for a long time!'

Suddenly, there was another burst of bright green light filling the deep inner space of the Planet Grigan. Ziob stood waiting patiently as the space became larger and larger. Brighter green luminous light now filled the enormously growing space.

Will saw people talking, walking, and laughing in their city of Epahs. Each building took on different geometric shapes. Will thought, 'I have heard the King of Spectron speak of buildings built in these strange shapes!'

As he stood watching the ever-growing city, he realised he had never seen anything like this before. He had never seen a city evolve before his very eyes like this. Will stood still, amazed, just watching the city grow larger and larger. There were thousands of people walking, working and talking to each other as the city grew.

Ziob said to Will, 'Follow me and I will introduce you to some other Space Masters.' Will did exactly as he was told.

As they walked closer to the people in the big city of Epahs, Will could see their faces. They smiled and nodded to him; he did the same back. Will noticed that these people, too, had a slightly greenish skin. 'Their skin isn't as lumpy and bumpy as the Griganians', though!' he thought.

Will and Ziob continued to walk towards and then into a building that had eight sides. Will instantly thought about his maths lessons at school: 'that is a regular octagon,' he realised. Will and the Space Master continued to walk up many flights of stairs within the building, into a very large library and what appeared to be a Hall of Learning where many other Space Masters, also dressed in green, were working.

These Space Masters were working with helpers. Ziob said to Will, 'The Space Masters work with their scribes. The scribes write on parchments.' The parchments, Will noticed, were the same size as the very large walls of the building. He also noticed some Masters working up ladders with their scribes working beside them!

In one area of the very large library, Will could see some people dressed in purple. They were so far away that he couldn't make out their faces. He couldn't help looking at these people, who really stood out next to the Space Masters and their scribes. Ziob was quick to see Will staring in their direction and said, 'My friend, our learning is open to all people who want to learn. We cannot deny them entry if they wish to join us.'

Will didn't know who these people were but he was soon to find out!

Chapter Four

Will Meets The Lizard People From The Planet Zadril

Ziob was very busy with some research she was doing. She introduced Will to her scribe, who was called Chet. Chet was always busy working for Ziob on projects, Will found out. The projects went from knowing how people use different languages on different planets, to how different planets work with their money and currencies and the different ways they use their money for trading, buying and selling, to the discovery of new planets and galaxies, and the different crops grown on different planets, and even more! The longer Will stayed with Chet the more he would learn, he realised.

Will was fascinated by all he was learning from Ziob and Chet and wanted to know more about the work they were doing. He asked, 'Why do you need to know so much?'

Chet looked in astonishment at Will. He thought before coming up with his answer. Then he rubbed his bony chin and replied, 'Why would you not want to know?' Will had not expected a simple answer; and the answer itself took him by surprise!

When Will looked in the direction of the purple people they had gone, vanished completely from the library.

Ziob and Chet also looked in the same direction. They, too, appeared surprised to see the purple people had left so quickly, thought Will. Chet quietly whispered in Will's ear, 'Those people are the Lizard People. They are from a very distant planet called Zadril; we don't know much about them!' Chet shrugged his bony shoulders as he made this last comment.

Chet, Will thought, could be mischievous; he always seemed to have a twinkle in his pink eyes. Strangely, Will felt very comfortable with Chet, and wondered at the vast work of writing he was undertaking. As Will looked from wall to wall and floor to floor, he could see that the walls were covered by Chet's work.

The library was a busy place with Space Masters and their scribes working hard. They were all searching for new knowledge and ideas, looking for new inventions and searching for new planets. Will became very busy reading one of the old manuscripts he found sitting on a green stone stool. He sat on the stool and started to read.

A passage in the book spoke of the Planet Zadril and the Lizard People. He read on, and as he did so, he couldn't believe what he was reading!

> 'The Lizard People were once a very wealthy and knowledgeable race. Through laziness, they forgot how to read and learn. Their laziness was so great that the Lizard People of

Zadril started to lose their respect for each other and for their planet.

'For generations the people have lived like this. They do not care about the planet or about each other and slowly there have become fewer and fewer people living and fewer babies being born on the planet.

'As space time went by, the lazy Lizard People of Zadril used up all of the natural resources of their planet. They do not go to school and cannot read; they do not know how to work; they cannot work out simple sums, and nor can they solve simple problems!

'The Lizard People of Zadril are dying and will not survive until they find the answers to life.'

Will thought about what he had just read and felt a sadness come over him for the purple people he had seen in the library and for the Planet Zadril. He felt he wanted to help these people and asked himself, 'But how can I help them when I'm only a visitor here on Grigan?'

Will looked up from reading and saw many Space Masters walking towards him. He jumped up quickly. They were dressed in long, flowing green robes and wearing green crowns on their heads, and each carried a bright green sword and large books that were throwing green light on their hands. Will suddenly dropped the old manuscript onto the floor. As it dropped, it broke into small pieces of brown paper and then slowly the brown paper crumbled into fine purple dust right before their eyes. All that was left of the manuscript was a small pile of purple dust sitting on the bright green shining floor of the Library in the city of Epahs!

The Space Masters of the Planets were now standing in front of Will; the very tall Senior Master looked at Will and then at the small pile of purple dust on the floor. He looked at Will again, and said, 'Welcome to Epahs, Will. I see you have been reading about the Lizard People of Zadril. It is very unfortunate, but they are stuck in the situation they are in.' He paused, and said in a matter-of-fact voice, 'It is all because they did not plan and work for their future; they have become a very lazy race!' He continued, 'Our children are becoming lazy too, and this is why we have brought you down to our inner city. We would like you to talk to our children and explain how you work on Ozimoth. Then we can speak to our children on different planets.'

Will felt very proud to be honoured with such a task. He looked at the Space Masters and said, 'Yes, I would like to meet and speak to the children of Epahs. Thank you for asking me.' Will was now so interested in the people of Epahs and the Space Masters that he had completely forgotten about the Grigan Leader up on the outer planet of Grigan!

Once the Masters had spoken to Will, they turned and walked away. Will, however, was still very interested in the people of Zadril and somehow, he knew he was going to help them. He walked to where the Lizard People had been working and studying. It seemed as though even the space he was standing in felt sad.

He was standing and looking around when a small purple Lizard girl came and grabbed his hand. He looked down and she said in a language that Will somehow recognised, 'Come with me, my people want to talk to you!'

The little Lizard girl was holding his hand very tightly, and she led him out of the Library and the Hall of Learning. After a time, thought Will, 'We seem to be walking and walking!' Finally he asked, 'How far are we walking and where are you taking me?'

The little purple girl looked up at him and replied, 'As far as it takes to meet my people!'

Will thought for a second and then decided, 'that answer told me nothing'!

They continued to walk and walk with the little Lizard girl continuously by his side. They walked over cold rocky and sandy ground. Will could feel the coldness of the inner planet on his skin. He glanced at the little girl still holding his hand; she too was looking very cold. Will thought about his clothes: he at least was wearing his jeans, trainers and a shirt, he silently thought to himself.

He looked at the little purple girl and suddenly realised, 'If I'm cold, how must she feel?' He then asked her, 'Aren't you cold?'

She was only dressed in an old, torn purple tunic and didn't wear any shoes. Will then thought, 'she must be very cold!' He thought again, quickly, 'I must concentrate on something else and not how cold I feel.' He asked the little girl, 'How old are you?' She just looked at him and didn't give him an answer. Then he thought again and asked, 'What's your name?' He found out she did have a name, when she replied, 'Eex.' Will pondered for a short time and then thought, 'That's a strange name!'

They continued to walk into the cold, deep moon time of the inner planet of Grigan. Eventually they came to a small cave. The cave was so small that the purple people Will met could only stand; they had no room to sit or sleep. He realised he had never seen so many people living in conditions that were as horrible as these. He looked at the Lizard People in the cave and could see the sadness in their very yellow eyes.

A Lizard woman came to meet Will and said, 'Welcome to our place on this planet. You can see how we are now living. However, we are here for a reason. We are here to learn how to work again. We need to learn how to look after our own planet and how to treat our people; we need to go home. There are many people waiting for us.

We need to take the knowledge we learn here back to our people on Zadril!'

Will looked at the people who were now all looking at him and said, 'Chet, the scribe to Ziob, has told me a little bit about you and your planet!'

The Lizard woman looked at Will through her squinting yellow eyes as he made his last comment. The eyes seemed to pierce his mind and this made him feel very uncomfortable. He thought quickly, 'Well, I suppose these are Lizard People.' He suddenly felt very mean and didn't want to think badly about any people. Will now politely asked the Lizard woman (as she stood watching and waiting for his next comment), 'What is it you want to know?'

The Lizard woman replied, 'We need to know how to grow crops, how other people look after their planets; how they live and how they work.' She continued, 'We would like to take you to our Planet of Zadril.'

Will replied, 'When?' in astonishment. The woman then said, 'We are going now.'

Will knew he should not go with these people but somehow knew he needed to. He thought for a moment and then agreed to travel to Zadril with them. The Lizard woman turned from Will, made a sign with her purple hand and the people turned and started to walk to the back of the cave. As light shone from the flaming torches they were carrying, Will could see the cave become longer and longer! He also saw that there were a lot more Lizard People than he at first had realised.

Will followed them. He then noticed that the little Lizard girl had been holding his hand all the time. She had never once let it go and was still holding his hand as they all moved further and further, deeper and deeper into the cave. Suddenly, they were leaving it. The Lizard People and Will were now in a very clear, cold, dry and barren place. Planetary winds were starting to blow and lumps of freezing ice whirled around their heads. It was colder now than before, the little Lizard girl was still standing next to Will, her hand still firmly in his!

The group lit more torches and Will could make out the faces of the Lizard People. He could also see the shape of what he thought resembled a spaceship. 'Or is it a spaceship?' he thought silently. From a distance, it looked very old, dented and rusty. Will could feel the panic in his body as he asked himself, 'Are we going to travel in that thing?' He almost said out loud 'That's just an old rust bucket!' At this point, he was not impressed with his decision to help these people!

The Lizard People started to board the spaceship. As Will came on board he could see the ship had wires and pieces of metal poking and hanging out of the walls. He could see pieces of wire dangling down from the engines and hitting people on their heads as they walked past. Will was a reluctant passenger and now, the last person to enter the spaceship. He looked around and couldn't help comparing this ship with the Grigan Leader's, or the King of Spectron's. Will could not help wondering 'How old is it?' And, 'Is it really going to fly through space?'

He looked at the inside and the rusty wires hanging from ceiling panels. He was now looking at the lights on the control panels; sometimes they would flicker 'on' but most of the time they would be 'off'. The more he saw of the inside of the ship, the more he noticed how dirty it was and how there was litter and rubbish piled up in the corners. He looked at the people he was now starting to travel with to an unknown planet! He started to question his own judgement at this point.

Will was now in a serious dilemma! He realised how the Lizard People, too, were very untidy and dirty. He was seriously wondering about this journey and asked himself, 'Have I really made the right decision here?'

Chapter Five

A Hazardous Voyage

Back on the outer planet of Grigan, the Grigan Leader had returned, looking for Will. Will was not there waiting for the Leader! Not even the very large hole in the ground could be seen; it had vanished. 'Will has completely disappeared from sight!' he thought.

The Grigan Leader scratched his lumpy, bumpy head in disbelief; he knew that Will would not have disobeyed him. Summoning his soldiers, he told them, 'We must find Will Jones. Search every building, every cave; ask every person you meet, knock on every door, we must find Will!' he ordered.

At the same time, deep down in the centre of Grigan, the Space Masters too, were looking through the city of Epahs for Will Jones. Ziob and Chet were very worried. After all, Ziob had brought Will to Epahs and the Senior Space Masters would want to know how and why he had disappeared.

* * *

Meanwhile Will's journey to the Planet Zadril had begun. The spaceship was making unsettling noises like, crank, crank, crunk, crank, crank, crunk, groan, groan; metal scratched against metal in a screeching, piercing sound throughout the journey!

Once in outer space, Will decided to take a look around the ship. Little Eex was still by his side, refusing to leave him. She somehow knew what he was interested in seeing. She took him to the control room where the Lizard People were trying to fly the spaceship and keep it on course. Again, crunk, crank, crunk, crunk, crunk went the engines; crank, crunk and crunk, groan, groan again, screech, crank!

Will was now scratching his head and thinking, 'I didn't even imagine that such old spaceships existed in the space worlds!' The spaceship and its passengers were somehow making their way through space to Zadril. At times Will wondered if they were ever going to get to the planet.

Eex was still by Will's side; she guided him to every possible place on the ship. At times he would have to jump over dangling wires and instruments that had fallen onto the floor from control panels. This spaceship did not travel at the speed of the Griganian or Spectron spaceships. 'By comparison,' Will thought, 'it's going a lot slower, in fact so very slowly, it's almost standing still!'

Eex had taken Will over almost every inch of the ship till, in the last corridor they went to, Will was introduced to many, many children. They were all waiting to meet him. Eex, too, was now very excited. She held Will's hand very tightly as they made their way, meeting the children and walking among them. Eex was very proud as she introduced her new friend to the children from her home planet.

The children too, were very happy and they all tried to speak to Will at once. The language they were speaking was a little different to the language that Eex spoke and Will found it difficult to understand them. He found he really had to listen to every sound and every word the children were making.

From the other end of the corridor beyond the children the purple Lizard woman walked forward. She looked at Will through her very yellow eyes. At this point, Eex also took the purple woman's hand. Will said to Eex, 'Is this your teacher?' Eex looked at the woman and then nodded back to Will.

Eex then slowly said, 'She is also my mother and the Queen of the Lizard People of Zadril.' Will remembered that she had spoken to him in the cave on Epahs. He also remembered that she had boarded the spaceship with the rest of the Zadrilian passengers. He couldn't help thinking to himself, 'She's not really dressed like a Queen, and doesn't look anything like the other Queens I've met.' He then suddenly realised, that Eex must be a princess!

The Queen then said in a very matter-of-fact voice, 'My name is Irdzla. You have heard about our planet and about how our people have become very lazy. I want to change the way we have been and now I want our children to have an education and a future place in the universe.'

The Queen had just finished what she was saying when, suddenly, the crank, crank, groan, bump, bump, bump and crank noises slowed down. The ship started to lose speed and it started to float in the space vacuum. The first engine, then the second, the third, the fourth, the fifth and lastly the sixth engine stopped! Will thought to himself, 'Oh no, the engines have died and now we are floating somewhere in outer space!'

Not a sound could be heard, it was 'as quiet and still as space could be!' thought Will.

The ship and the passengers were now floating. Will knew that, because of the lack of gravity in outer space, with no engines working they could float in space forever! He had experienced floating through space before and was now used to this feature of travelling. Will thought, 'This is fun, but it isn't going to get us anywhere. We need to start the spaceship's engines again.'

He had an idea; guiding and pulling his body along the panels of the spaceship with his hands, he floated to the engine room. He remembered seeing dials and wires hanging out of the rusty walls of the ship and knew that they should not have been just hanging as they were. He found the dials hanging from pieces of wire and looked round for something that could be used as a screwdriver. He found a piece of metal with a flat shape now slowly passing him in space and thought 'That should do the job, I think!'

He was now very busy trying to repair the dials and looking at where the loose wires belonged. Even the dials and wires were rusty. As he tried repairing the dials some of the wires broke into many pieces in his hands! He couldn't help thinking and muttered to himself, 'That's how old all of this technology really is!'

All this time, Princess Eex was there by his side. She too, was floating and appeared familiar with the experience. She wanted to help. She floated around the engine room collecting pieces of wire and dials from mid-air, and all the things that she thought would help Will. She then arranged them carefully so that they became easy for Will to find as he worked on repairing the spaceship.

Queen Irdzla of Zadril had also floated to where Will was working; she watched him work and then made herself busy copying how he mended and fixed pieces of wire and dials.

Will had really enjoyed engineering, metalwork, electronics and technology at school. He thought, 'This old spaceship is very different to the engines of cars and boats and motor bikes that I've worked on with my dad!'

As Will worked, he spoke to the Zadrilian Queen, saying, 'Your Majesty, may I ask, were you teaching the children when Princess Eex and I came into the corridor?'

She replied, 'Yes, I was.' She continued, 'When I saw you in the Library at Epahs I knew that you had come to guide us.'

Will listened to what the Queen was saying while he continued to work, fixing the loose wires, and putting the dials back into the spaceship wall. He was thinking carefully and wondering how a short visit to Zadril could help to make up for many, many moon and sun times of laziness by the Lizard People. 'Or is it going to be a short visit?' he pondered.

Will, Eex and Queen Irdzla were now working very hard. Slowly some of the Lizard People gathered around them. Will showed them what he was doing. They too, found loose wires and fixed them back to dials and other pieces of the spaceship's engines. The Lizard People started working all over the ship. They were fixing and mending dials, cleaning the machinery. Some of the Zadrilians even started to tidy up the spaceship by picking up the rubbish, Will noticed.

As the last loose wire was put back into its place, the ship's engines started to make a noise, crank, crank, whir, crank, crank, whir. Will had not heard the familiar sound of whirring before on this old ship, but now he listened carefully, and thought 'Oh, I think I can hear the sounds of a proper spaceship's engine!'

As the Queen heard the sounds of the engines come to life, a very large smile came across her purple face. Little Princess Eex too became excited.

The spaceship travellers slowly started to find their feet again. They came down from floating to walking around the ship. The spaceship slowly picked up speed and now started to speed through space.

They passed many different planets, planets of many colours, some of magnificent size, and slowly on the horizon Will could see a purple planet emerging. He wondered, 'Is that the Planet Zadril?'

The Queen joined him and said, 'You asked if I was teaching the children when you came into the corridor, Will.' She continued, 'I was teaching the children the value of whole numbers, multiples and odd and even numbers, and how to multiply numbers. Would you like to see what I was teaching them?'

Will was impressed with this and said, 'Yes, I would'.

Queen Irdzla and Will walked to the end of the ship's corridor. The Queen showed him the brown, dirty parchments on which she had written the lessons. Slowly and carefully unfolding the very old parchments, that had been used time and time again, Will noticed, the Queen tried to make the figures clear but because the parchment was so old it was difficult for her to do so.

EACH NUMBER HAS A VALUE.

THE SIZE OF THE NUMBER DEPENDS ON ITS VALUE.

EACH COLUMN CHANGES VALUE BY A FACTOR OF TEN.

TEN MILLIONS	MILLIONS	HUNDRED THOUSANDS	TEN THOUSANDS	THOUSANDS	HUNDREDS	TENS	UNITS
						7	3
					2	9	7
				4	3	5	4
			2	3	1	5	8
		3	1	6	4	3	0
	1	1	2	3	1	2	4

ROW 1) SEVENTY-THREE
ROW 2) TWO HUNDRED & NINETY-SEVEN
ROW 3) FOUR THOUSAND, THREE HUNDRED & FIFTY-FOUR
ROW 4) TWENTY-THREE THOUSAND, ONE HUNDRED & FIFTY-EIGHT
ROW 5) THREE HUNDRED & SIXTEEN THOUSAND, FOUR HUNDRED & THIRTY
ROW 6) ONE MILLION, ONE HUNDRED & TWENTY-THREE THOUSAND, ONE HUNDRED & TWENTY-FOUR

The Queen explained, 'The Space Masters allow us to use their Library. This is a way we can learn. If our children and our people are to survive, they must be educated and they must know how money works.' She then showed Will another old parchment and said, 'It's very important that the children understand the differences between odd and even numbers.'

She continued, 'I have written the odd numbers in red and the even numbers in blue.' Queen Irdzla continued looking through the old brown parchments on the floor of the spaceship, talking to Will as she did so. 'Our children need to understand that we must learn to trade with other people. We have many precious stones and minerals on Zadril that other planets do not have.' Will looked at the Lizard Queen; he could see the kindness in her bright yellow eyes and knew, somehow now, that he wanted to help her.

She had yet another dirty old parchment she wanted to show him and this parchment was teaching the children how to multiply numbers.

She said, 'Our children need to know these sums; they are the multiplication or times tables up to 10. I was teaching them how these numbers work when you came into the rridor with Princess Eex.' She turned away for a moment and said, 'While I talk to Will, children, see if you can work out what 7 times 6 comes to. After you've done that, what is 4 times 9?'

	1	2	3	4	5	6	7	8	9	10
1	1	2	3	4	5	6	7	8	9	10
2	2	4	6	8	10	12	14	16	18	20
3	3	6	9	12	15	18	21	24	27	30
4	4	8	12	16	20	24	28	32	36	40
5	5	10	15	20	25	30	35	40	45	50
6	6	12	18	24	30	36	42	48	54	60
7	7	14	21	28	35	42	49	56	63	70
8	8	16	24	32	40	48	56	64	72	80
9	9	18	27	36	45	54	63	72	81	90
10	10	20	30	40	50	60	70	80	90	100

She continued talking with Will as she looked though the brown, dirty parchments with her work on them. At that point Queen Irdzla said, as she held up the table from one to ten in front of Will, 'Our children need to know how to buy and sell things. If our children learn these tables it will help them when they need to learn how to multiply and divide numbers, and when they need to add many numbers together.'

Will now stood with his hands in his jeans' pockets and said, 'Well, I couldn't agree more, Your Majesty!'

He then thought for a while. He knew there were wise beings in the solar systems and on other planets and in other galaxies and knew they would want to help the Queen if they only knew how much she wanted the children to learn. Will looked on as the Queen continued to explain the lessons to him.

He nodded his head; he knew, now, he would have to do something to help her, 'but what?' he wondered.

The old spaceship was now closer to the Planet Zadril and Will could see the looming size of it. The Queen and Princess Eex, too, were now looking through the ship's cracked and dirty windows at the planet ahead of them. Only now did it occur to Will, 'Oh, we have to land this thing. I had forgotten about landing. I just hope the ship makes it!'

As Will watched, the closer the ship came to landing; he could see and thought to himself, 'Run-down buildings and a planet that looks as though it has just been through a war!'

As the ship docked the door very slowly and reluctantly opened. The shrieking hinges were forced to move, allowing the door to open so that eventually the passengers could leave the ship.

When the door was completely open, Will could see, everywhere he looked, that the buildings were run-down, rubbish all over the place and things were dirty and broken.

Far over the horizon, though, he could see the colours of blue and green. It looked as though these colours were a long way off and over many hills and mountains, but he thought, 'I can see the familiar colours of Grigan, Spectron and Ozimoth!'

He had temporarily forgotten about his home and Ben. He suddenly thought, 'Oh dear, I've forgotten all about Ben. I was to meet him and I'm now out somewhere in space. I can't even text him!' He felt for his mobile phone in his jeans' pocket and remembered, 'Drat, I left my mobile phone at home this morning!' He then thought again, 'I couldn't even text Ben from here anyway.'

As the Lizard People left the spaceship it swayed from side to side, squeaking, moaning and groaning under their weight. Will thought, 'This thing will disintegrate at any moment!' But it didn't, it remained in one sorry spaceship state. He was thankful for that. Queen Irdzla and Princess Eex were the last to leave the spaceship. They were both busy picking up the precious brown parchments from the dirty ship's floor. Will hastily helped them collect all the parchments the three could carry!

Given all of his surprises so far, Will was not surprised by what he experienced next!

Chapter Six

Will Learns More About The Planet And People Of Zadril

The Lizard People were walking about the streets of the city of Lardiz. They were not happy people. Will couldn't help thinking, in fact, how miserable they looked. They were very scruffy and dirty and nobody seemed to care about anything, he thought.

The streets were dirty with litter and had rubbish in every corner. Wherever he looked there was litter! Will thought quietly, 'I don't think I've ever seen so much rubbish, or a place so dirty!' The buildings were also dirty, with broken windows and doors hanging off their hinges. The trees in the streets were dead and a heavy dust lay over everything and every street!

Will followed the Lizard Queen of Zadril and little Princess Eex as they walked towards a very large brownish building. The people who had travelled from Epahs were not like the people who had stayed on Zadril. The travellers were now happy, chatting and talking and enjoying their conversations. 'They don't seem anything like the people here on Zadril!' thought Will, then thought again, 'But the travellers were like these people before they started working on the spaceship!'

Queen Irdzla and Princess Eex walked with Will into the big brown building. Will assumed that this was the Queen's palace. It too, was scruffy and nothing like the palaces he had visited on other planets, he quietly realised.

The Queen wanted to talk to Will. They walked through many large, dirty, deserted and dusty rooms. Will noticed that long couches and chairs were torn and battered and covered in dust, and very large Xannnt webs hung from the ceilings and doorways. As he was walking through the rooms, Will saw many Xannnts, large eight-legged creatures with very large nippers and beady eyes on the ends of their tentacles. Will was to later find out that Xannnts are fierce and 'bite you hard if you don't watch out'!

He realised they were watching him as he walked; now, he too watched them! He thought, and then said out loud, 'I hope I don't get one of those in my bed!' Queen Irdzla and Princess Eex both smiled at his comment.

At last they came to a room at the back of the building. When the door was opened, it revealed a large room that was very clean and very neat; it was clearly the Queen's apartment. Princess Eex left them and came back a little later 'looking more like a princess!' thought Will. The Princess was holding the hand of a younger boy child. She told Will, 'This is my Little Brother; he is more than 2,000 suns younger than me!'

Will was impressed. 'She may not know her own age, but she knows her brother is so much younger than she is!' he quickly realised.

The Queen gave the little Lizard boy a kiss and sat in a high, grand chair with the child on her knee. Speaking to Will, she said, 'Please take some refreshment!' At that moment, an elderly Lizard butler came into the room carrying a tray full of drinks in strange looking glasses, and platters of different fruits, and square-shaped biscuits that were covered in a type of chocolate sugar. Will thought, 'those biscuits look too delicious not to eat!'

As always, he wanted to try the different foods he came across and the biscuits looked to him like perfect eating. They were so tasty that he couldn't stop eating them, and apologised for eating so many. 'I am sorry to be so greedy,' he said, with a mouthful of biscuit, 'but these are truly delicious!'

Queen Irdzla now wanted to talk again. With a full stomach, Will was ready to listen. She explained, 'Here, in the palace gardens, we grow some vegetables and crops, and we also grow a chocolate bean. My Lizard People cannot be bothered to grow anything and wouldn't ever have eaten like you have just eaten!' She continued, 'As you can see, our city is run-down and dirty. The people do not want to work; they don't see any reason to work. They are unhappy and they want better things and a better life, but they think these should be given to them. I know that all of us need to work to get our city and our planet back to the way it was in the time of our great, great, grandparents.

'Our people think that, because their ancestors worked hard to create the wealth and opportunities in the past, they don't have to continue to work now!

'I have spoken to them, but they cannot see that they need to work to maintain our city, work in the fields and farms and develop learning in our children for the future. They also need to work for themselves and each other.'

The Lizard Queen was frustrated and angry, Will realised. As he thought about the Queen's statement, he too was amazed at what she had just said. Queen Irdzla waited patiently for him to say something in reply to her statement.

Will thought for a space moment. He deliberately did not make a comment about the Queen's remarks. His reply was, 'Your Majesty, when the spaceship was coming in to land, I saw in the far distance, over many hills and past many mountains, the colours of blue and green. What is that land?'

The Queen thought about her reply, then said, 'That's the land of the Zarwids; we are not permitted to enter that land.'

Will wanted to know more and asked, 'Who are the Zarwids?' He continued with his questions, asking 'Why are you not allowed to enter that land?'

Queen Irdzla again thought for a short space time and then replied, 'They are the Wise Ones of Zadril. They predicted that, because we had such a wealthy and plentiful land, we would one day, through laziness, go the way we are going. We did not take any notice of the Wise Ones and now they refuse to help or talk to us. Yet I know they are very wise and they may hold the secrets that will help us to repair our cities and help our people!'

Will was very interested in the Zarwids and wanted to know more about these Wise Ones. He wished to ask more but, somehow knew, now was not the right time. He thought, 'I remember the change in the Lizard travellers after they had helped to repair the spaceship.' He also thought about the children growing up with Lizard parents who did not care about anything, and who thought they should be given everything. He thought, 'If these people have a chance to work, and if they could see the changes it brought, surely they would want to change the way they are now?'

He then wondered, 'Would the parents want to work or not? Would they want a better future for their children?' After thinking for a short space moment, Will said, 'Your Majesty, do you think it would be best for you to go to the Wise Ones and speak to them?'

The Queen thought about Will's question, then replied, 'Do you think that would help us?'

With a very matter-of-fact tone to his voice, Will replied, 'You can only ask them for their help. They can either say "Yes" or "No", Your Majesty!'

Queen Irdzla again thought about Will's suggestion and then replied, 'Yes, we will go to the Zarwids and ask them for their wise suggestions and their advice. Will, I would like you to come with me.'

Will nodded his head in reply. He knew he was not in a position to say 'No'; he also knew that now he was going to meet the Zarwids in the land of blue and green. He kept his thoughts in silence. This prospect he found very exciting!

While the Queen made arrangements for the journey, Princess Eex showed Will some of her sums and arithmetic scrolls and parchments. She explained, 'I could only use the digits once to make the numbers in this scroll. First I had to make the largest number possible, and then the number closest to 40,000.

'Once I had thought about it, it was as easy as seeing a shooting star, and these are my answers.'

TEN DIGITS MAKE ALL OUR NUMBERS. THEY GO FROM ZERO TO NINE, LIKE THIS:

0, 1, 2, 3, 4, 5, 6, 7, 8, 9

THE LARGEST NUMBER USING EACH DIGIT ONCE WOULD BE: 98,765

THE NUMBER CLOSEST TO 40,000, USING EACH DIGIT ONCE, WOULD BE: 39,876

Will was very impressed and asked, 'Princess Eex, who taught you to do these sums?' The Princess replied proudly, 'My mother!'

Princess Eex wanted to show Will more and more but it was time for him to travel with Queen Irdzla to the land of the Zarwids. Will turned to say 'Goodbye' to Princess Eex, but just at that moment the Princess had brought into the large room even more pieces of dirty parchment and scrolls with her work written all over them. Will smiled at her and said, 'I will look at them when I return.

I will be back to see you!' As he left the room, Will felt sad for little Princess Eex. He thought, 'She just wants to know so much, and she is so eager to learn everything!'

Will and the Queen now left the brown, drab building. Will had wondered how they would travel to the land of the Zarwids. He was soon to find out. Waiting for them at the end of a dry and dusty road were two strange-looking animals. They looked a little like horses, but they weren't horses; 'They look much stronger than horses!' Will thought. They had large heads with long manes hanging over their eyes. They also had long fur hanging all over their bodies and legs. The Queen explained, 'These animals are from the mountains. They are called Gupse and have many powers; they can do many things!'

The Gupse were saddled up and Will noticed that they carried many blankets. Queen Irdzla told him to mount the Gupse, which he did; he then realised, 'I've haven't done much riding lately and this Gupse is a lot wider than the horses I ride on Ozimoth!' Will felt his legs stretch as he managed to mount and sit comfortably in the saddle.

Both Will and the Queen were now ready to leave Lardiz. They trotted down the dusty, dirty streets to begin their journey. Will could feel the power of the Gupse as they started their journey. No sooner were they out of the city than the Gupse started to gallop like the wind. The Queen shouted to Will, 'Hold on, you are in for a ride!' Will noticed a slight giggle in her voice, and looked back at the Queen, whose Gupse was a little distance behind.

The Gupse were now galloping, and as they picked up speed, they left the Zadrilian ground and climbed higher and higher. As the Gupse climbed their wings unfolded from within their furry bodies. Both the creatures and their passengers were now gliding through the air on their journey to the Zarwids.

As they travelled, they climbed higher and higher. It was getting colder, in fact, so cold that the Queen shouted to Will, 'Put some of the blankets round yourself!' She hurriedly wrapped herself in many of the blankets.

They were now flying into blizzards and fierce winds. As Will wrapped the blankets around his body, he was surprised at how warm they were. He hadn't realised the natural Gupse hair blanket would be so cosy. He shouted to the Queen, 'I'm as warm as toast, now I have the blankets wrapped around me!'

They travelled from moonrise to sunset, and again many times. As they travelled they passed over many tall snow-capped mountains and when Will looked down from his seat, high on the back of the Gupse, he could see mountain rivers and what, he thought, were many different seas below in the far deep-down distance. Will was now starting to feel weary. He had eaten a lot of food at the Brown Palace and the warmth of the blankets made him feel sleepy. He realised this, and thought, 'I must stay awake; if I don't, I may fall off the back of the Gupse!'

He was finding it difficult not to fall asleep and slowly his tiredness became too strong; he could feel his eyelids shutting and his head slowly moved forward onto the neck of the Gupse. Then suddenly, he was startled wide awake. A great white light was there before him, becoming brighter and brighter.

He looked and stared, but could not see what was happening. They were now changing direction: 'The Gupse are almost going around in circles!' he suddenly realised. Will found it difficult to hold onto the Gupse. He did not understand what was happening or where they were going. He just hoped they would somehow land safely. He tried to see Queen Irdzla but could not. He called her name. No answer came back.

'She's vanished in mid-air!' Will thought. All sorts of ideas now started racing through his mind.

Chapter Seven

Princess Eex And The Butler Meet A Messenger

Meanwhile back at the Brown Palace in the city of Lardiz, Princess Eex was making herself busy; she was determined to do as many mathematical problems as possible before Will returned. She looked for clean parchment but there was none. She knew there were some old parchments that had been used in the time of her great, great grandparents, and these parchments, she remembered, were down deep in the dungeons and vaults of the Brown Palace.

Her mother had forbidden her ever to go down to the dungeons, and Princess Eex knew she would be in big trouble if she went there alone or, indeed, if she went there at all! It was, after all, the burial site of her ancestors and '….should not be disturbed', her mother had always said.

Princess Eex pleaded with the elderly Lizard butler to go with her to the dungeons to find the parchment she needed. 'Please, Butler, please come with me,' she begged him, over and over.

He would continually reply, 'We will both get into very great trouble if we go into the dungeons: you know that, Princess Eex.'

She was so persistent that, in the end, he had little choice but to go with her down into the deep, dark dungeons. They walked to the stairs that would take them down and under the Brown Palace.

They walked down and down. It was dark, smelly and damp. Xannnt webs were hanging thickly from the vaulted ceiling. Everywhere the pair tried to walk, their heads would knock into another thick, sticky Xannnt web! These would stick to their faces and their necks, and to their hands as they tried to remove the web.

Luckily the elderly butler had had the brains to take a lamp with him. Princess Eex felt like turning back but her will to find the parchment was too strong: she would not give up her search for parchment now she had started, she thought.

Going down the winding stairs Princess Eex again started to feel a bit frightened about the journey she was on. She looked around and saw shining pairs of Xannnt eyes peering at her. Xannnt nippers were snapping as she continued to walk down and down the stairs. One of these fierce creatures was so close to her ear that she heard, snap, snap, snapsnap and snap again!

At last they were down as far as the stairs would let them go. From the foot of the stairs corridors went off in eight different directions. Each direction was another long, oval corridor, she noticed. The butler did not know which way to go. He thought to himself, took a guess and then said, 'Princess Eex, let us take the fourth corridor; I feel that one will be lucky.'

They both walked forward into the dark, smelly, mouldy corridor. The light from the lamp flickered, then went out. They were there now in pitch darkness, deep in the bowels of the palace, and could hear the continual snap, snap, snap of the Xannnt nippers never stopping to take a break.

Princess Eex felt really frightened now. The butler held her hand tightly and said, 'Don't worry, Princess Eex, I will light the lamp again and then we will be able to see where we are going!' The Lizard butler did just that; the lamp wick was again alight and they could very clearly see the size of the enormous corridor they were standing in!

They walked and walked; the corridor appeared to have no ending; there was nothing in it but larger and larger Xannnts. Some Xannnts were almost the size of Princess Eex. The elderly Lizard, seeing how large the creatures were getting, thought it was now a good idea to turn around slowly and walk back to the stairs. Snap, snap and snapsnap went the nippers of the Xannnts, again and again.

At last they were safely back at the stairs. Princess Eex considered returning to the Queen's apartment upstairs but then thought of the reason she had come all the way down to the dungeons. 'I need to find some parchment to do my sums and work on,' she thought. She looked up at the elderly butler and said, 'I think we should go over there,' pointing her purple finger, 'down that corridor.'

This was the darkest corridor of them all. Even the elderly butler was not too sure about that corridor. Princess Eex felt him shudder, as he stood beside her. He really didn't want to walk that way at all, she realised.

The light from the lamp was now showing them the way into the deep, dark corridor. It was very, very dark; the light from the lamp flickered. They walked into the blackness and, as they walked, they could see many different shapes before them. Large Xannnts were everywhere, hanging down and climbing over the shapes!

Princess Eex looked again at the shapes and then asked the butler, 'What are those?' He was still holding her hand tightly and said, 'I believe they may be your ancestors, Princess Eex, but I'm not sure!'

Princess Eex had remembered her mother saying, 'Your ancestors should not be disturbed. They have a right to rest now, Princess Eex.'

The Princess thought for a bit and felt a little guilty. She said to herself, 'I don't want to disturb my ancestors, but I do need the parchment I came down here to find!' She kept her thoughts from the elderly butler. She was now leading the way, looking for the parchment she needed so badly.

At the end of the very dark corridor, she saw a pile of papers, writings and books. She let her hand fall out of the butler's and ran to them. 'There is so much paper and parchment here!' she said to him.

She couldn't believe it. She started to move books and stood looking at some very ancient parchments she had picked up from the floor.

The elderly butler was now by her side; he too was busy looking at the dusty piles of papers, books and writings. He picked some papers up. As he did this, the papers, because they were so old, crumbled in his hands and the crumbs and dust from the parchments fell to the floor!

Princess Eex didn't care any more about the Xannnts that were starting to gather around her; she was just interested in what she had found. She turned to speak to the elderly Lizard and was about to say, 'We will take all...' when she suddenly fell silent. The butler looked round, in the direction that Princess Eex was staring. Standing there before them was a very large knight or king. Princess Eex was not sure who he really was, but she knew he was somebody important, she thought to herself.

She had heard her mother speak of '...Space Beings and the Intergalactic Space Masters from the Council of Space Elders'. The Princess knew the Space Masters must have great powers. If that is what he was, this one was dressed in a dazzling white robe with a crown of rubies and stars upon his head. He had long white hair and held a sword of shining light.

The butler fell to his knees and then the being spoke. 'You do not have to bow before me; I'm here as a messenger from King Lagrieb.'

The Lizard butler knew that King Lagrieb is the Highest Elder King, Overseer of the Space Masters and Space Messengers and the President of the Intergalactic Council of Elders. Princess Eex had never seen any being so bright before; she stood in front of the Space Messenger, her mouth open wide, and just stared at him.

The being then said to the butler, 'You must help Princess Eex all you can. You will find the parchment you are looking for. Search a little harder; it is waiting for you.' In an instant the magnificent being had gone. He had delivered his message to the elderly Lizard butler and the Princess and that is all he had been ordered to do!

The butler was now unable to think clearly for a space moment; he scratched his bald head and stroked his purple beard, and then set to work.

He searched between the old documents and manuscripts, looking for parchment that Princess Eex could use. As he touched most of it, it fell to crumbs and pieces in his hands. For some reason, his glance fell in the direction of one of the ancestors whose 'mummified' head appeared to be looking at him.

He felt a shudder go down his spine as he looked at one of the Kings of Ancients' past. He thought, 'I may be wrong, but I believe I just saw the eyes of the Ancient moving and twitching.' He looked again, and said out loud, 'By the Planet of Zadril, I do believe that's old King Lexif, looking at me!'

When he realised that this old king of many generations past might have come to life, the butler felt like running to the safety of the stairs, but he did not. The elderly butler walked slowly and cautiously to the place where the Ancient Ancestor was standing in his burial casket, nodded his head in respect and looked down at the ancient's feet.

All of the time Princess Eex watched the elderly butler. She, too, now felt frightened; she said nothing; she just watched and waited. There, in front of the casket, suddenly appeared before them piles and piles of clean, white, gleaming parchment. It just kept appearing. Every bundle was tied with golden and purple ribbons. There were now bundles and bundles of parchments, and as Princess Eex stood and watched, more and more parchments appeared. Every one was tied with golden and purple ribbons!

She thought, 'There is so much parchment that I will have enough to use for the rest of my life!' She thought again, 'All of the Lizard children will now have parchment!' She was so happy: she had never seen parchment like this. All of her work had been done on old parchment that had been used time and time again. She ran to the ever-growing pile of parchment and took rolls and rolls of it into her arms – all she could carry!

She then said, 'Butler, please carry as many of these as you can up to the palace, and then we shall come back for more. More and more! We will keep coming back until we have carried it all upstairs.' She spoke excitedly.

With every trip they made, despite picking up parchments and taking them up to the palace, the piles in the dungeons grew bigger. Every bundle was tied with the same golden and purple ribbons. The piles of parchment, in the dungeon, continued to grow. Princess Eex now knew that she would have enough parchment, not only for herself, but for all the Lizard children on the Planet Zadril and for their future learning!

Princess Eex suddenly stopped as she picked up another roll of parchment from the floor and realised: 'The parchment is so very fine, clean, white and shiny. It is by far the finest parchment in the universe!' She realised then, 'The paper feels fine and smooth; it is nothing like the rough, old, brown parchment I have always used to do my work on!'

The piles of parchment just continued to grow, pushing the Xannnts out of the way as it overtook the space in the deep dungeons of the Brown Palace of Lardiz. By the time the suns went down, Princess Eex and the butler were exhausted from continuously carrying the parchment up the long, high stone staircase to the palace. Once they had finished for the moonrise, Princess Eex, instantly, and within that very space moment, started working on the clean parchment. As she worked, she felt her energy return!

She worked very hard, thinking, 'I have no time to waste. I want my mother and Will to see my work on this very nice, clean and shining parchment!'

The elderly Lizard had walked up and down the palace stairs for many space hours carrying bundles of parchment up to the Queen's apartment. When they had finished, he gratefully sat down in his comfortable brown stone seat and watched Princess Eex and her brother work. He didn't sit quietly for very long before his eyes closed and he fell into a deep sleep.

Princess Eex and her brother continued to puzzle out and write down their work. Princess Eex's Little Brother thought he would show Will how he worked with his sum tables and this is what he did:

He worked hard and had completed the two and three sum tables and was now working on the fourth sum table.

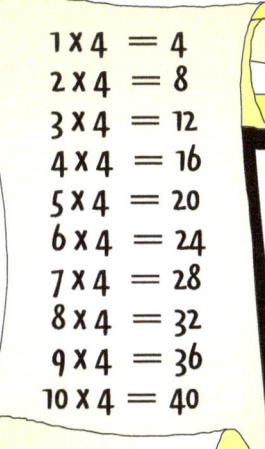

He had also been working on a maths problem that turned out to be a little bit harder than he had thought it would be. He was quietly thinking to himself, 'I will show Will how these sums are done!'

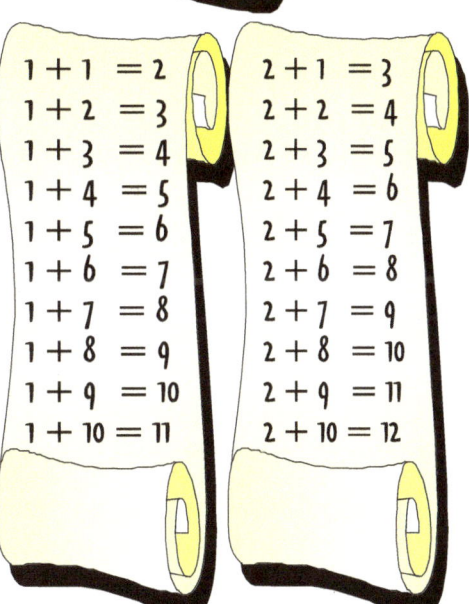

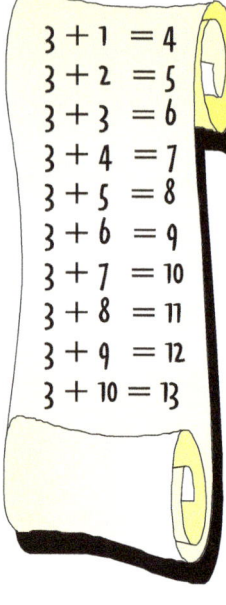

Princess Eex and Little Brother continued to work; still the butler slept. Little Brother created this sum table. The sums are a little different; can you spot the difference?

Princess Eex's Little Brother had hated his sums lessons with his mother, but now he could see how numbers can become magical. He could also see how useful sums could be, he thought, as he worked, lying on the brown stone floor of the palace. Look at the following numbers; can you see the magic that Little Brother has just seen?

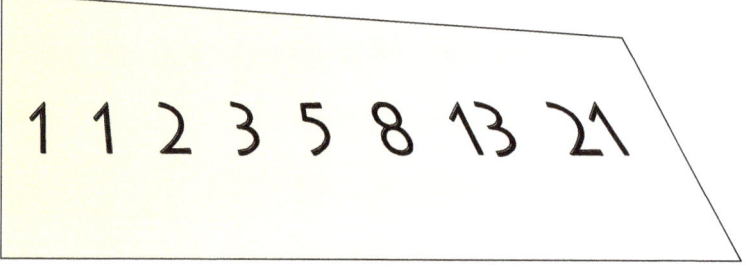

Would you be able to work out what the next number will be after 21?

Each number is the total of the previous two, so the next number is 34! The Queen had taught both of the children these magic numbers. Princess Eex's Little Brother enjoyed watching numbers grow just like this. Here are some more magic numbers. Princess Eex's Little Brother pushed the sum on the new white parchment across the floor to his sister and said, 'Sister, find the missing number!' Can you find the missing number?

$$2\ 4\ —\ 16\ 32\ 64$$

Princess Eex thought and after a while said, 'Eight'. She then said, 'Now do some more; see how many magic numbers you can manage to get onto one piece of parchment.' Little Brother now started to work really hard. This is his work. Can you spot the patterns in the numbers? They are all different, so be careful!

$$3\ 6\ 12\ —\ 48\ —\ 192$$
$$4\ —\ 16\ 32\ —\ 128\ —\ 512$$
$$160\ —\ 40\ 20\ —\ 10\ 5$$
$$25\ 20\ —\ 10\ 5$$
$$8\ 13\ -\ 23\ 28\ —\ 38\ 43$$

As the children were busy working great columns of green thick light spiralled over the Brown Palace, then disappeared as quickly as they had come.

Princess Eex continued to work on her sums. She thought, 'I have so much to do before Will returns!' Meanwhile the elderly Lizard butler stayed fast asleep in his comfortable, brown stone chair.

Princess Eex was determined to complete as much work as she could. 'I have never had such good, clean paper to work on!' she thought excitedly. She remembered the multiplication tables (times tables) her mother had been teaching her. She decided to work the sums out her way and this is what she did. She asked herself, 'What are six twelves?' then wrote her answer down, just like below.

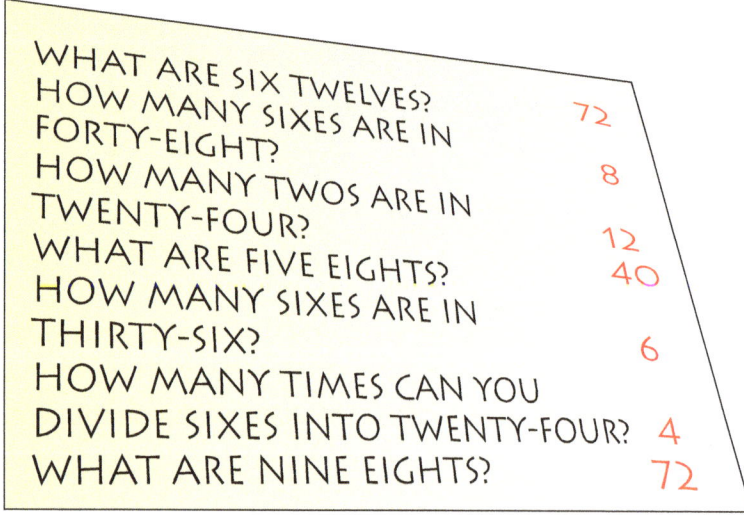

Princess Eex wanted to do more and more of the sums that her mother had taught her. She started working on another clean and gleaming parchment.

While she worked, she kept by her side the old brown parchment on which her mother had worked out the multiplication table. She occasionally looked at it and thought of her mother, Queen Irdzla.

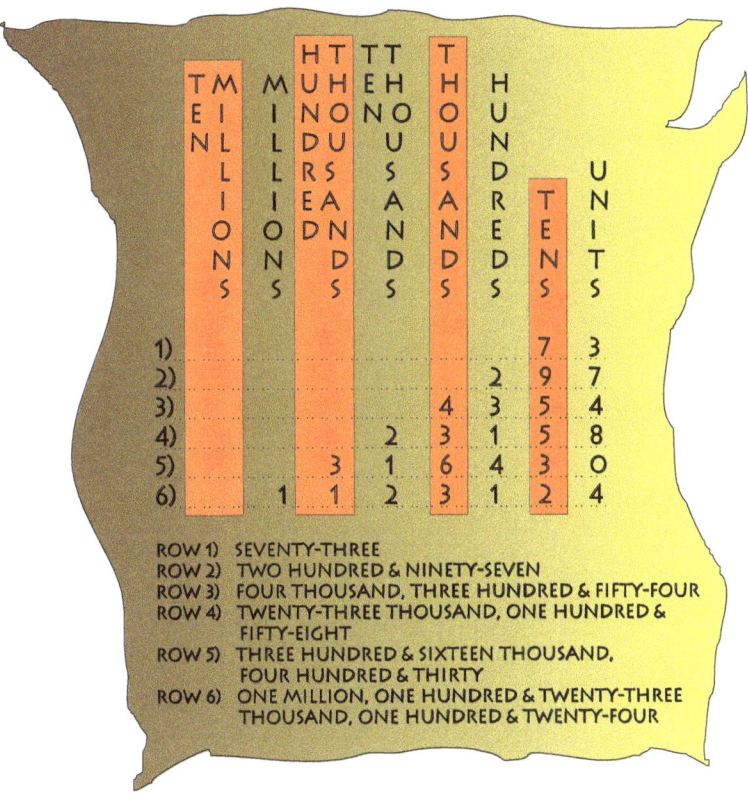

ROW 1) SEVENTY-THREE
ROW 2) TWO HUNDRED & NINETY-SEVEN
ROW 3) FOUR THOUSAND, THREE HUNDRED & FIFTY-FOUR
ROW 4) TWENTY-THREE THOUSAND, ONE HUNDRED & FIFTY-EIGHT
ROW 5) THREE HUNDRED & SIXTEEN THOUSAND, FOUR HUNDRED & THIRTY
ROW 6) ONE MILLION, ONE HUNDRED & TWENTY-THREE THOUSAND, ONE HUNDRED & TWENTY-FOUR

Princess Eex continued to write and work out mathematical problems. She wanted to stay very quiet; the Lizard butler was still fast asleep. She thought to herself 'I don't want to wake him, he has worked very hard this sun-up time!'

She continued to work quietly, writing:

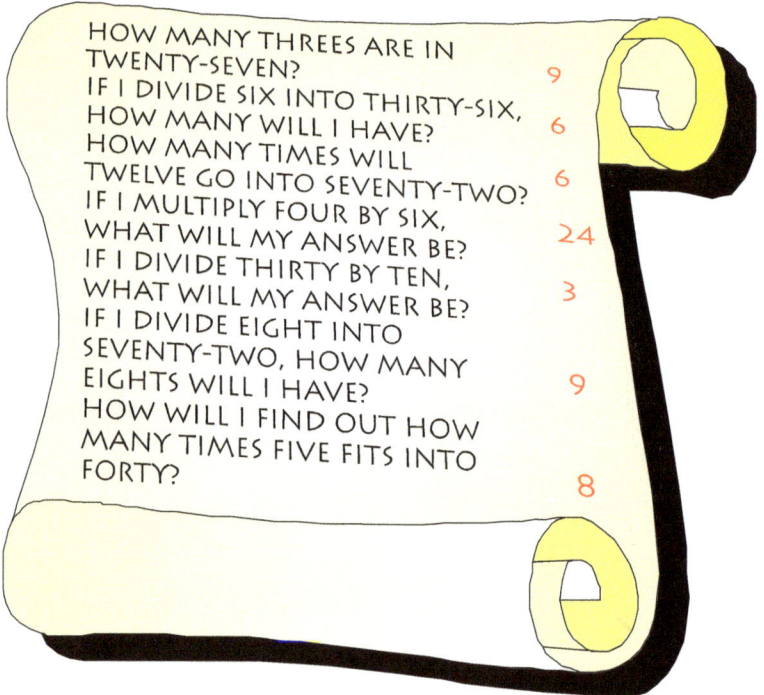

HOW MANY THREES ARE IN TWENTY-SEVEN? 9
IF I DIVIDE SIX INTO THIRTY-SIX, HOW MANY WILL I HAVE? 6
HOW MANY TIMES WILL TWELVE GO INTO SEVENTY-TWO? 6
IF I MULTIPLY FOUR BY SIX, WHAT WILL MY ANSWER BE? 24
IF I DIVIDE THIRTY BY TEN, WHAT WILL MY ANSWER BE? 3
IF I DIVIDE EIGHT INTO SEVENTY-TWO, HOW MANY EIGHTS WILL I HAVE? 9
HOW WILL I FIND OUT HOW MANY TIMES FIVE FITS INTO FORTY? 8

Princess Eex was so very busy she did not see the columns of thick, green light come into the large brown room again and surround the three of them!

The columns of light whirled and turned and weaved through the room. Around the sleeping butler they went, weaving in and out. Through his legs, over his body, around his head and still they wove their eerie green light! All of the time the Princess and Little Brother continued to work on their maths puzzles.

* * *

While the children in the Brown Palace are working, Will and Queen Irdzla are on a hazardous journey to find the Zarwids!

Chapter Eight

The Planetary Storm, And After

Will continued going round and round in the tunnels of wind; he was still on the back of the Gupse. The winds became colder and colder. He found it hard to look, to see where he was going. The further he fell the more difficult he found it to open his eyes because his eyes stung so much with the cold air almost freezing them! He was now starting to feel sick, '…very sick,' he thought, '…very sick indeed, in fact!'

He could not see the Queen: she had completely disappeared, Will suddenly realised. The Gupse was bolting and whining like a wild, menaced horse; it too was very frightened as they became giddy in the tunnel of the fierce winds. Will and the Gupse went spiralling and spiralling down; it was like being inside a whirlpool or tornado, Will felt. He was trying to think. He said to himself, 'Maybe it's like being in a washing machine when my mum washes the clothes!'

Suddenly, bump, bump, b-bump; they were now both on the ground: Will and the Gupse! Will hit his head on something hard. All he remembers is feeling the knock on the head and then seeing stars and circles just before he lost consciousness.

* * *

Slowly he felt his thoughts come back into his head. He was lying on some warm straw in the middle of a room. As he looked around he noticed the walls had no corners; he then realised he was in some sort of round room. He stayed very still, as his head was still very sore and it was even sorer if he moved it. He touched his scalp with his fingers and carefully patted the sore patch. He could feel the lump growing as he touched it. He then felt the 'thump' of pain begin. His head was so painful he could only lie very still on the warm, clean straw and rest. Every time he tried to lift his head, he had to rest again. 'My head's just too sore to move!' he now realised.

As he lay there he thought of the Gupse and then Queen Irdzla. He thought, 'Oh my gosh, whatever has happened to her?' He tried to get up from the warm straw and, as he did so, his body fell back down again. He was too weak, at this point, to move and knew he could only lie there on the soft, clean, warm straw and rest. He thought to himself, 'I will have to wait until I feel better before I try to get up again!'

Slowly he felt his eyelids close; he tried to stay awake but his eyelids became heavier and heavier until he could not open them any longer!

He slept and slept. He was not aware of where he was or what was happening to him. He had no idea of what had happened to the Queen or the Gupse. He knew nothing of their whereabouts.

After many moonrises and sunsets, Will started to feel his body again. He could not open his eyes and as he tried to do so, his body seemed to ache even more. He thought, 'I will just have to wait until I'm well.'

He lay thinking about Queen Irdzla and '...how I must find her'. Slowly and very carefully, after a great rest, he opened his eyes. He couldn't recall how long he had been asleep but realised, it had been a long, long time. Slowly, as he opened his eyes, he looked around the round room and saw many, pairs of eyes looking back at him.

He wanted to get up off the nice, warm straw in a hurry but his body was still aching and he was still very weak. He would now have to wait and see what was to happen next, he thought. He looked around and started to see who it was that owned the eyes that were looking back at him.

Will had never seen these people before. They had very green, shiny skin. It shone so much that they were almost transparent. They had green eyes and red lips. They were all wearing green tunics and Will looked at them again. He remembers thinking, 'their clothes are made out of large green leaves stitched together!' He was surprised at this, he recalls. As he lay on the warm straw he asked, 'Have you been looking after me?'

A taller green person came into the round room and spoke to Will. He was dressed in rich green leaf robes and wore a crown of green leaves upon his head. He said, 'You have been sleeping for much time. You are now almost well.'

Will looked at him and said, 'Thank you for looking after me. Where am I and who are you?'

The green tall leader said, 'I'm King Tanure. We are the keepers and guardians of the Planet Zadril. We are the Nature People of this planet. Our mission is to protect the planet and to keep it safe. King Lagrieb has given us this task,' he continued.

On his last visit to Spectron Will had heard the King of Spectron speak of King Lagrieb. He knew that this was the President of the Intergalactic Council of Elders of the Universe. Will now asked the King, 'Do you know if Queen Irdzla of the Lizard People is safe?'

The King looked at Will and said, 'Yes, she is safe and like you she has been getting well. You were both caught in a planetary snow and swirl storm. You are lucky that you landed in the field of leaves otherwise some other fate might have been waiting for you!'

Will then asked, 'And the Gupse, are they safe?' The King looked at Will and said, 'Would you like to see them?'

Two of the King's aides helped Will to his feet and they walked towards the door of the small round room. There in the distance and through the trees, Will could see the Gupse in a meadow of rich, shining green grass that was swaying in the planetary breeze. He strained his eyes to see them and laughed and asked, 'Are they eating that nice, fresh grass?' He then continued, 'They look very happy out there and a lot fatter than when I first saw them in Lardiz.'

The King looked at Will and gave a hearty laugh and replied, 'Eat! They have done nothing but eat. They don't know how to stop eating. Don't you have any grass on your part of Zadril?' he asked.

Will shook his head as if to say 'No.'

Will was starting to feel much better now and he found he could stand by himself without anybody holding him up. He touched his head and found the lump; it was still very large but much smaller than he remembered. The King called a name and a beautiful green Nature Woman came into the round room. She had long flowing green hair and wore a gown and crown of many-coloured leaves and bright native berries.

The King then said, 'This is Queen Narute. She has been looking after you. She will put some of this bees' curd on your head and the swollen lump will start to disappear.'

The Queen placed some of the bees' curd on a sweet scented leaf and gently patted the curd onto the lump. When Queen Narute had finished, Will could almost feel the lump disappearing. He touched his head again and the lump was completely gone. He also felt very well, in fact. He thought and then said out loud, 'I could jump over our Earth's moon right at this moment, I feel so good!'

He then composed himself and waited for the King to suggest a meeting with Queen Irdzla. The King proposed the meeting immediately! Will was now ready to the see the Queen. He was hoping she felt as well as he did.

The whole party left the small round room in the middle of the trees and walked towards another larger round room. Queen Irdzla was sitting in a chair made from leaves and dried grasses. She looked up as the large party came into her room.

She looked at Will and a broad smile spread across the purple face of Irdzla, the Lizard Queen of Zadril. She tried to get up from the chair and quickly fell back down again. Will and two of the King's aides rushed to help as she stumbled. She was now safely back and sitting in the leafen chair.

She said, 'Will, you look so very well. I understand you have been sleeping for many moonsets and sunrises.' She then asked, 'Do you feel well enough to continue our journey?'

Queen Narute heard this and begged the Lizard Queen not to travel so soon, saying, 'Your Majesty, you are still recovering. To undertake such a journey so soon would not be wise!'

Queen Irdzla thought for a space moment and said, 'We will wait until the next moon has gone into grey time and then we will travel.' She continued, 'We need to speak with the Zarwids.' King Tanure and Queen Narute stood listening to Queen Irdzla as she continued to speak of their mission. 'We urgently need to ask for the advice of the Zarwids.'

King Tanure and Queen Narute looked at each other. They could hear the plea in the voice of the Lizard Queen. The King replied, 'We will help you to speak to the Zarwids. They will give you wise information and knowledge.'

Will then looked at the Lizard Queen of Zadril as she sat in her leaf-and-grass chair. He thought '…the Queen looks very tired, it will be good for her to rest here for a while longer, before continuing our journey.'

Slowly, the large party of Nature People, the King and Queen, and Will left Queen Irdzla to rest and get well, ready for the next part of the journey to the Zarwids.

Chapter Nine

The Green Light And Princess Eex

Meanwhile in the City of Lardiz, Princess Eex and Little Brother were still doing sums, and the elderly butler was still asleep in his comfortable, brown stone seat. By this time, the children had so many sheets of gleaming, white parchment completed that they were covering the floors of the Queen's apartment. Princess Eex was busy doing additions, subtractions and multiplications. She turned to speak to her Little Brother and said, 'If I take three Xannnts away from five I will have two left over.'

Princess Eex's Little Brother stopped what he was doing to look at her work. She then said, 'If I have fifteen Xannnts and take eleven away I will have four left over.' All of the time she was drawing Xannnts and her sums looked like this:

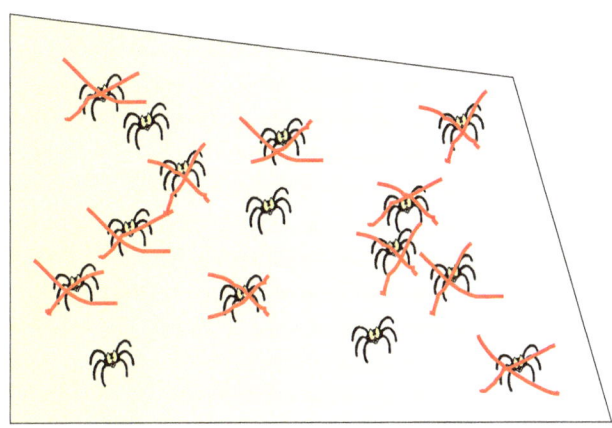

Princess Eex's Little Brother continued to watch her working and listen to her talking.

She said, after a space moment of thinking, 'If I have nineteen Xannnts and take seventeen away, I will have two left over.'

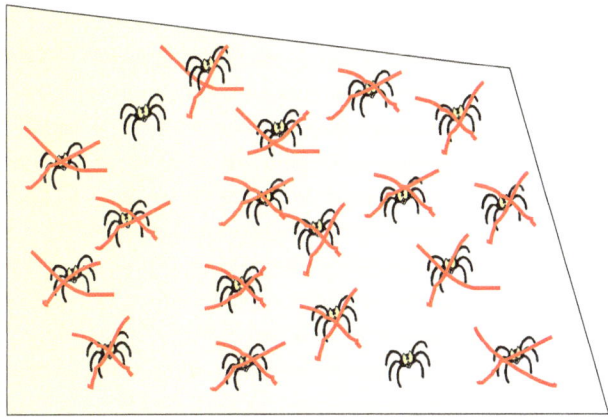

She now drew another twenty Xannnts. Princess Eex's Little Brother, by this time, was becoming very sleepy.

He, too, fell asleep, resting his purple head on a pile of pure white parchments on the brown stone floor. All of the time Princess Eex continued to draw Xannnts and count in addition and subtraction. She said quietly, as the butler and Little Brother slept, 'One, two, three, four, five, six, seven, eight, nine, ten, eleven, twelve, thirteen, fourteen, fifteen, sixteen, seventeen, eighteen, nineteen, twenty.' Then she said, 'If I take five away from twenty, I will have fifteen left.' She was about to say…?

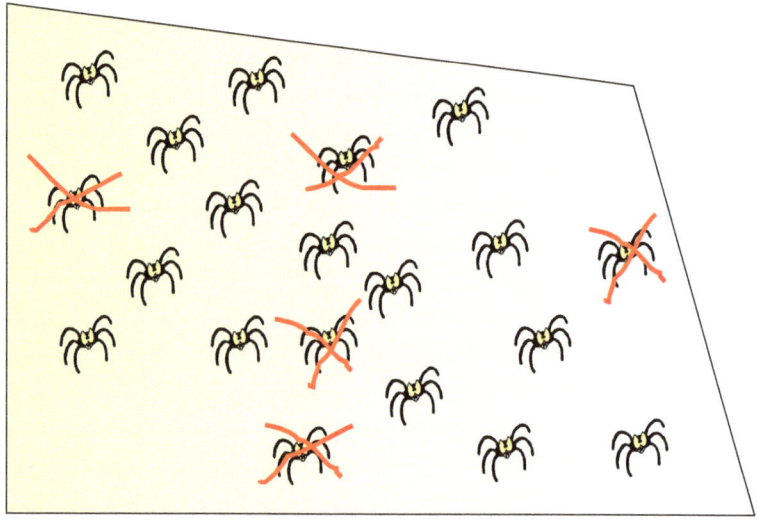

Suddenly, the thick green light was swirling round and round her again. Princess Eex could feel something touching her skin. She started to become frightened. As she looked down, she saw the shape of a green hand appearing, touching her and holding her small, purple arm! She was just about to scream when suddenly, standing there before her, a green being appeared from out of the swirling, thick, green light. The green being wore a green robe, a green crown upon her head and carried a brightly coloured, glowing green sword in her hand. She said, 'I am Ziob, from the City of Epahs. Please do not be frightened, little Princess Eex, we are looking for Will Jones.'

Princess Eex was now standing and her work was left on the brown stone floor. She was still holding her drawing stick in her hand. Swirling green lights were now gliding and winding all around the Queen's apartment.

Princess Eex felt a little happier to hear the green woman speak her name. She replied to Ziob, 'Will is with my mother. They are travelling to the Zarwids to ask for help and wisdom.'

Then Ziob nodded her head in approval of this news and replied, 'Ah, that is a very good idea!' She continued, 'When do you expect them to return?'

Princess Eex replied, 'I don't know but I know I'm trying to do as many sums and mathematical parchments as I can, to show Will when he returns.'

She was trying to act very brave and grown-up but she could feel her knees shaking as she spoke.

Ziob was impressed with little Princess Eex. All this time, the butler and Little Brother slept soundly.

Princess Eex bent down and looked through the parchments she had been working on, then again spoke to Ziob. 'I would like to show you these sums. I have done them on this very nice clean parchment.'

Ziob moved forward and looked at the little Princess's work. She was impressed by what she saw. Ziob put down her sword and sat down on the brown stone floor with Princess Eex. The Space Master looked on at first, then they started to work together. Ziob looked at Princess Eex and said, 'I think you have worked very hard on your maths.'

Princess Eex knew she had worked hard and she thought to herself, 'I've never had nice clean parchment like this to do my work on before!'

All of the time the spiralling green lights were weaving and moving through the Queen's apartment. Princess Eex was no longer aware of the green lights. She was only aware of the new friend she had found in Ziob. They both began to work very hard on the maths parchments. The first thing they worked on was a little parchment for Little Brother to complete. He is to count the number of planets on the parchment!

Princess Eex drew Xannnts on the next parchment. She drew groups of Xannnts. Can you see how many Xannnts are in each group?

The next parchment that Ziob and Princess Eex worked on has to do with money. Ziob asked Princess Eex, 'Do you have money to buy the things you need?'

Princess Eex had heard about money, but they didn't use it on Zadril, so she said, 'I know a little bit about money, but I don't really know how to use it!'

Ziob looked up into the high brown ceiling of the palace, touched her chin with her green finger and thought about her answer carefully; then said, 'Well, in the City of Epahs, where I live, we use money to buy the things we need.' Ziob continued, 'Another word for money is currency.

'I am a Space Money Master and I work in the Treasury of Epahs, where I have to make sure that we only spend the money we have in the Treasury.'

She continued, 'We have many Space Masters on Epahs. We all have different projects to control and look after.'

Ziob took a deep breath and continued, 'Because I look after the money of Epahs, the government of Epahs pays me money in return for my work.' Ziob thought for a bit and said, with a giggle in her voice, 'Funny that, isn't it? I'm paid money to look after money!' Princess Eex looked at Ziob's face and realised that even Ziob was a little confused about being paid money to look after money!

The Space Master went on, 'I have to make sure we pay our bills, and that we have enough money, and that we don't run out of money: and that's my job!' She stopped and thought again, then continued, 'I have to balance the books, so to speak!

'The Space Masters are always searching for discoveries; sometimes we watch the planets, or study the people of other planets, and we learn about the way they live, and how they work and survive. We learn about how they farm their land, and how they look after their farm animals, and how they grow their crops...'

Ziob had so much to tell Princess Eex, but knew she would run out of space time sooner rather than later. Princess Eex was very interested in what the Space Money Master was saying. She sat on the brown stone floor, her legs crossed and stayed completely still while the Space Master told her many stories about different space people and how they live on other planets.

Ziob continued, 'On other planets, when the space people work for the King or Queen or the government, the government pay those people for the work they have done.'

Princess Eex had never heard of this before and asked 'What is pay?'

Ziob continued to explain, 'Pay or payment is given to you if you work for somebody or for the government. For instance, if I said to you, "Princess Eex, we must pick up all of these parchments before your mother comes back to the City of Lardiz." You would do that and not get paid.' Then Ziob asked Princess Eex, 'Do you understand that?' Princess Eex then said, 'Yes, I think I do.'

Ziob carried on, 'When you become a Queen and you ask one of your citizens to clean the streets, if you do not offer them payment, they will not want to clean the streets, so your city will become dirty.'

Ziob then asked again, 'Do you understand that Princess Eex?'

Princess Eex thought for a short space time and said, 'Is that why our streets are so dirty?'

Ziob was careful with her answer; she too, thought for a short space time, then said, 'It may be so!' Ziob thought '…now would be a good time to change the subject and move on with the conversation!' She said, 'I'm going to show you how our money system works in the City of Epahs.'

Princess Eex was very interested to learn more about money and how people on other planets earn it and work with it. Ziob could now see the interest in the face of the little Princess. Ziob started to speak, and drew, on a piece of clean, gleaming parchment, '…how the people of Epahs use their money system.'

She drew some coins like the ones they use in Epahs, and explained: 'You will need to know what these coins are worth.' She continued, 'When something has worth, we then say it has a value.' Ziob stopped, took a deep breath and said, 'That may be a little difficult for a young Princess to understand!'

Princess Eex did not move; she listened to every word that Ziob was saying. She then replied, 'You mean that if I value something, I will pay money to buy it?'

Ziob was astonished at this very intelligent answer! She replied, 'Goodness me, Princess Eex, you learn very quickly!' Realising how intelligent the little Princess was, she quickly said, 'I will tell you now about decimals. A lot of planets are now working with them. A decimal is one-tenth or one part of ten or ten parts of a hundred.' Ziob then asked Princess Eex, 'Do you know how to count to a hundred?'

Princess Eex nodded her head and eagerly replied, and said excitedly, 'Yes, yes I do.' She started counting, 'One, two, three, four, five, six, seven, eight, nine, ten, eleven, twelve, thirteen, fourteen, fifteen, sixteen, seventeen, eighteen, nineteen,' and stopped to take a breath. Ziob then quickly said, 'Very good, you know your numbers,' instantly stopping Princess Eex from continuing to count the rest of the numbers to one hundred. By this time Princess Eex was getting excited and said eagerly, 'My mother taught me my numbers.'

Ziob nodded her head and said 'That's very good. Shall I continue and tell you about decimals?'

Princess Eex again nodded her head, giving Ziob permission to start explaining.

Ziob said, 'In Epahs, a shape is the whole amount and, if we have one hundred parts in our money, we have one shape to spend.' She said again, taking a deep breath, 'We use parts and shapes as our money in the City of Epahs.'

Ziob then asked Princess Eex, 'Do you remember another name for money, Princess Eex?'

Princess Eex replied, 'Currency!'

'Good,' replied Ziob. 'This is how parts and shapes work in our decimal currency. One "P" equals one part,' pointing to one of the coins she had drawn, 'two "P" equals two parts, five "P" equals five parts, ten "P" equals ten parts, twenty "P" equals twenty parts, fifty "P" equals fifty parts and one hundred "P" equals one hundred parts. One hundred parts are equal to one shape.' She then asked 'Do you understand, Princess Eex?'

Princess Eex then said, 'So do two fifty parts make one shape?' Ziob answered, 'Yes, that's correct and well done.' She was clearly very impressed by this answer from the little Princess.

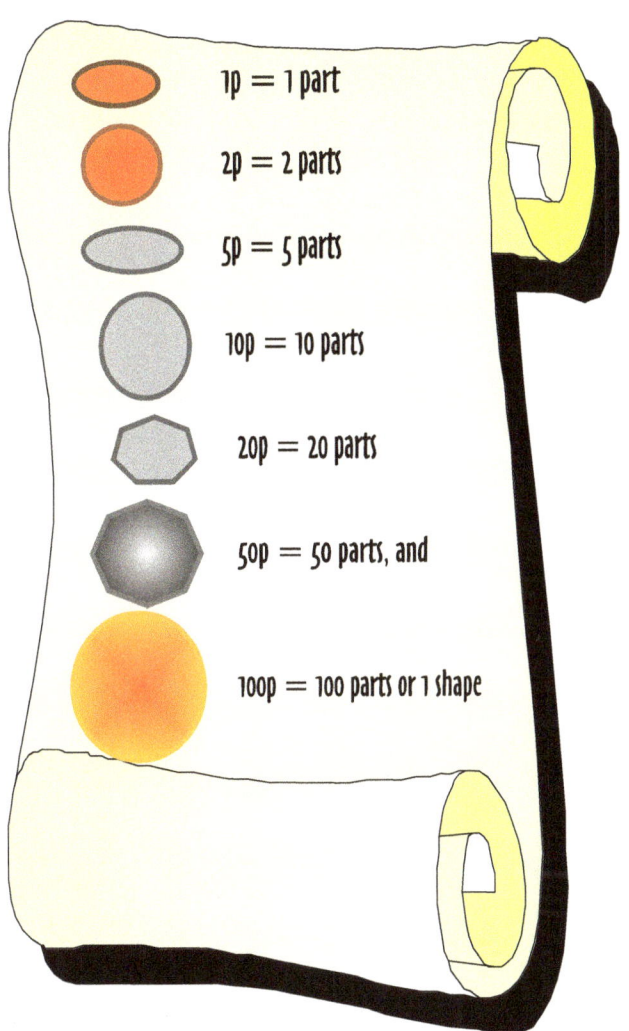

Princess Eex sat on the floor fascinated by what Ziob was telling her. Princess Eex thought for a space moment and then said, 'How do your people get this money?'

Ziob, too, thought for a space moment, then replied, 'We work and get paid for the work we do!' She continued, 'Let's do another parchment so that you can see how we start to use our money!' She unrolled a parchment and drew more coins, telling Princess Eex to 'watch the number of coins and start counting the parts within them'.

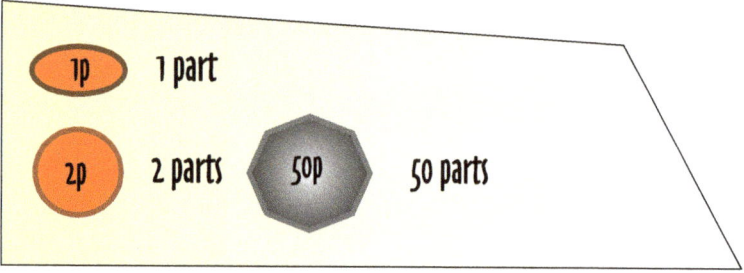

Ziob counted, 'One part, two parts and fifty parts.' She then asked Princess Eex, 'How many parts are drawn on the parchment altogether?'

Princess Eex said eagerly after counting, 'Fifty-three parts.'

Ziob nodded her head and said 'That's very good; let's do another one.' She unrolled another clean, crisp parchment to work on. Princess Eex was so excited she had forgotten about her Little Brother and the Lizard butler, still fast asleep! She had also forgotten about her mother the Queen, and about Will. She now just wanted to learn from Ziob.

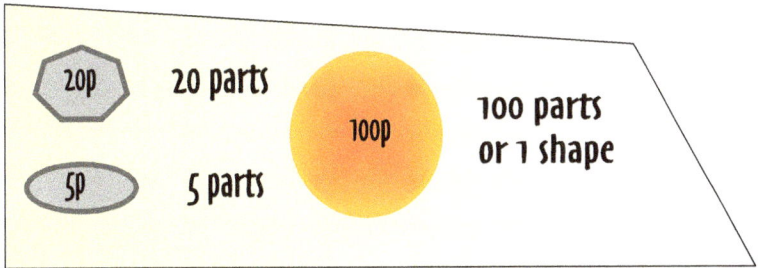

Ziob now asked, 'How much money have I drawn on the parchment?' Princes Eex took a space moment to think. She held out her eight green fingers and two green thumbs and said, 'I haven't got enough fingers to count all of the parts!' She thought a little harder and continued, 'One shape and twenty-five parts or one hundred and twenty-five parts.'

Ziob was now very impressed and said, 'Well done, we will do one more parchment.'

All of the time the two were busily working the thick bright green lights continued moving and gliding over and around the Queen's apartment. Princess Eex was still not aware of the bright, green lights; she was just too busy working to notice anything at all!

Ziob unrolled another fresh, clean parchment and drew some money again. This time it was drawn differently. As she drew, she said to Princess Eex, 'Now watch these parts and tell me the answer when you have worked them out.'

Princess Eex looked at the number of coins on the parchment and counted them. This is how she does it.

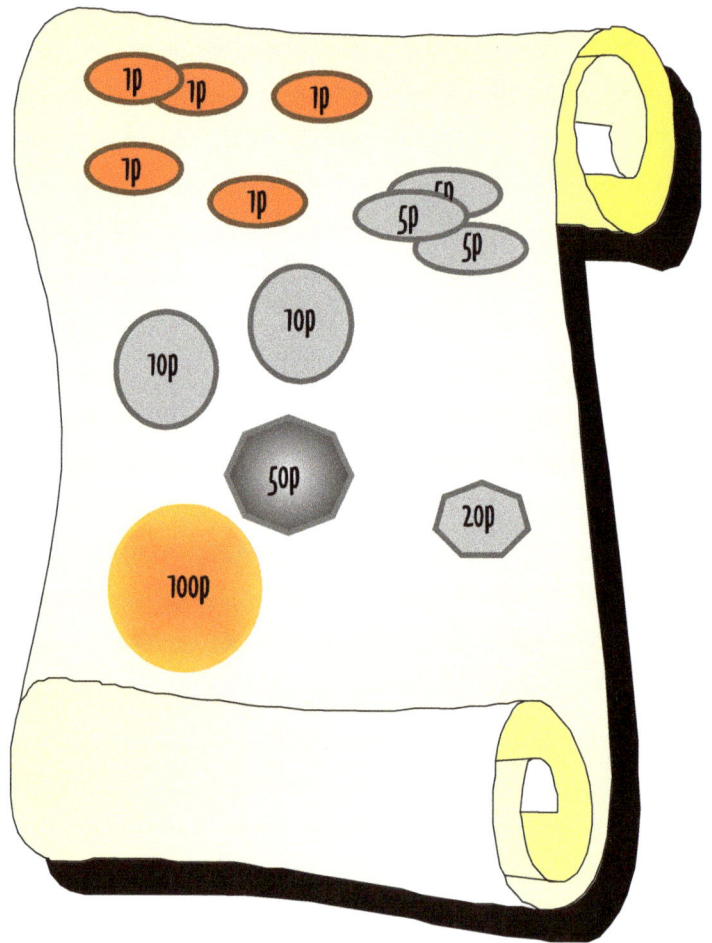

She counted and said, 'There are five one part coins, so that makes five parts altogether;' then wrote the number five down on a piece of parchment. She then said 'There are three five-part coins,' and went on, '...this makes fifteen.' She now wrote fifteen down on her parchment; then said, 'There are two ten-part coins: that makes twenty parts.' She wrote the number twenty on the parchment as well. Then she said loudly, 'There is only one fifty-part coin, one twenty-part and one one-hundred-part.' She now had all of these numbers written down on the parchment.

Her parchment looked like this:

5 lots of 1 P which equals 5P,

3 lots of 5P which equals 15P,

2 lots of 10P which equals 20P,

1 lot of 20P which equals 20P,

1 lot of 50P which equals 50P,

1 lot of 100 P which equals 1 shape.

Ziob looked at her and waited for the answer. Princess Eex was very quick to add them up and said, 'There are 210 parts altogether. Or two shapes and ten parts.'

Ziob, listening, thought, 'I am more and more impressed by this little Princess!'

Just in that space moment the thick green lights came down and surrounded the Princess and Ziob.

'Zap,' 'zap,' the green lights went, round and round Ziob and the Princess, 'zap,' 'zap,' again. Princess Eex spun around and around, following the lights in the Queen's apartment. Ziob, too, was spinning with her: round and round they spun!

Suddenly Princess Eex landed on the brown floor; she was alone; Ziob had disappeared. Princess Eex looked everywhere to find her friend but was now completely alone with Little Brother, the elderly butler (both still sleeping) and her parchments of work. She looked for Ziob but Ziob had vanished, almost, she thought, 'Into outer space!' Suddenly, she felt very tired indeed and, curling up next to Little Brother, fell sound asleep.

Chapter Ten

The Giant In The Mountain Pass

When she woke up, Princess Eex could not tell how long she had been asleep. She looked at the work she had done with Ziob. She continued searching for Ziob, 'but she is nowhere to be seen!' thought the little Princess.

She suddenly heard a sound behind her. At first she thought, 'It must be Ziob!' It was not. It was Little Brother and the elderly butler, who were now waking up themselves. She looked at Little Brother who was rubbing his sleepy eyes with his purple hands. He looked at the pile of parchments on the brown stone floor and asked, 'Did you do all that work while I was asleep?'

She replied, 'Yes, well, somebody helped me!'

Little Brother didn't appear to understand what she had just said. She also felt, she didn't want to explain any more about what had happened with Ziob. The Lizard butler was also awake and looking at the pile of parchments. He said, 'Princess Eex, you have been busy!' He then looked at the money parchments and said, 'I remember money. We used to use it, and it made working much more enjoyable!'

He realised what he had said and hoped that the children didn't really understand his comment. Nonetheless, he thought quietly to himself, 'It was nice to be appreciated and to be paid fairly for what I did.' He thought for a space moment and wondered how Princess Eex could know about money? He didn't feel he needed 'to ask any questions at this space moment in time!'

* * *

Meanwhile, Will and Queen Irdzla were on their journey to find the Zarwids. They had said 'Good bye' to King Tanure and Queen Narute in the forest and were now galloping on the Gupse towards the lands of Blues and Greens.

'These were the lands I saw from the spaceship window,' thought Will.

After leaving the leafy forest they had to pass through some very high, treacherous mountains. The Gupse were very strong animals; they were used to cold winter weather, snowstorms and blizzards. The two explorers had travelled through most of the mountains and were drawing closer to the Blue and Green lands; but they did not expect what happened next!

Suddenly, there in front of them on the mountain pass, stood a figure so tall and so strong that they could not pass him. Will had not seen such a vast creature before and asked the Queen, 'Is this a giant, Your Majesty?' The Queen did not answer Will. She too, did not know of any person so large that lived in these mountains.

The giant wore a tunic of fur and carried a sword and a shield. He wore a helmet of metal upon his head and a cloak of blues and greens around his very large shoulders. He started to address the Queen. His voice was so loud that it deafened Will, the land shook and the seas and lakes bubbled! The Gupse became nervous and started to bolt upwards into Zadrilian air and down to the planet's surface again. Will and the Queen found it difficult to keep the animals from turning round and running back from where they had just travelled!

The giant stranger bellowed, 'I am the keeper of the lands of Blues and Greens. Why are you here?'

Once the Gupse had settled back down, Queen Irzdla dismounted from the creature and went to speak to the giant. As she stood in front of him, Will suddenly realised how small the Lizard Queen was when compared to the giant. She did not even reach as far as his knees!

She said in a gentle voice, 'I am Queen Irzdla of the Lizard People and the City of Lardiz. I have come to speak with the Zarwids; I need to ask them for their advice.'

The giant looked down at the tiny Queen. Will was now very worried. He knew that with one movement of the giant's leg the Queen could be killed. As Will was thinking this, the giant started to shrink in size. He became smaller and smaller until he was the same height as Queen Irzdla. The Queen was very humble and waited for the keeper to speak.

The ex-giant replied to the Queen, 'You have chosen a very difficult journey; you must be very distressed to make the journey you have attempted.'

The Queen replied, 'Yes, I am very concerned about the Lizard People and the City of Lardiz.'

The giant then said, 'You must follow this mountain path and only travel straight along the path.' He repeated, 'You must not take another path; you must stay only on the straight path.'

The Queen listened to the keeper and then, once he had said what path they should follow, he instantly disappeared. All that was left was a small puff of smoke where the keeper had once stood. Queen Irdzla looked back at Will and said, 'Did you hear the message the keeper gave me?'

Will replied 'Yes, Your Majesty.'

The Queen remounted the waiting Gupse and they started on their journey again. They had only travelled a short distance when the path curved into a luscious green forest. Will called to the Queen, 'Your Majesty, this is not a straight path; we must not follow that path.' With Will's call, the Queen headed her Gupse into an unseen track and from nowhere, there in front of them, there appeared a very straight path. The curved path into the inviting forest simply disappeared in the mist of the mountains. They must now be on the right track, Will thought.

They travelled into grey time and there, in the far distance, they could see the lights of a village.

As they travelled, the village came closer and the grey time became colder. To get to the village they needed to turn to the right. The Queen asked Will, 'Do you think we should head to the village, Will, for shelter during the very cold grey time?'

Will replied, 'That will take us off the straight path which the keeper told us to stay on.' It was getting colder and colder, but Will remembered the blankets the Gupse were carrying and said to the Queen, 'Your Majesty, remember the blankets: we should wrap them around ourselves and then we'll be warm.' The Queen and Will did just this and instantly, the village to the right disappeared. There was no village there at all, just a test to see if they would obey the keeper. They travelled on through the deep grey time and stayed warm and cosy in their blankets.

It was now sunrise and the travelling party were very tired. They saw a stream running to the left of their pathway to a cool lake in the distance. The Queen asked Will, 'Should we go to let the Gupses drink, Will?'

Will replied, 'I think we should stay on the path and not go to the lake.' At his words the cool lake disappeared and there right in front of them on the straight track was a sign on the road reading, 'Welcome to the Land of Blues and Greens'. Will wondered if this was another trick and decided just to keep travelling along the straight path.

They now entered the Land of Blues and Greens; it was exactly as the sign had said. The land was as green as green could be, with trees, many types of coloured birds and butterflies, flowers growing, and insects flitting from tree to tree and flower to flower. A mighty ocean could be seen in the distance and, as Will listened, he could hear the sound of running water. The crystal-clear waters were waterfalls running between the trees and rocks, the grass and flowers. Will looked around. He had never seen a land so beautiful, he thought.

Waiting to meet them were the Zarwids. Queen Irdzla was welcomed to the Land of Blues and Greens by Empress Zidwar. She was a young woman and around her ascended every colourful butterfly and bird that had ever lived. The young Empress said, 'Welcome, Queen of the Lizard People. You are searching for the answers to help restore the City of Lardiz and your people to the prosperity of your forefathers and mothers.'

The Queen hadn't expected the Zarwids to know the reason for her journey and she replied, 'You are right!'

The Zarwid Empress then continued, 'The answer is simple: you need to give back to your people the gift of life: the gift of self-respect, dignity and self-worth; and then you will see your people change.'

The Queen did not understand what was meant. She asked, 'What do you mean, "the gift of life"?'

Empress Zidwar answered her, 'Your people need to work but they must be rewarded. Your ancestors would pay the people for the work they did. For generations the leaders of the City of Lardiz have not paid for the work that was done by the people. Your people now have no heart to work; they have lost "the gift of life" and that is why you must change the way you work with your people.'

' "When people work they must be rewarded!" ' Queen Irdzla repeated the Empress's words. She now understood what was said to her and knew that she must return to the City of Lardiz and make instant changes. The Queen said, 'Thank you for your wise words. Come, Will, we must straight away return to Lardiz!'

Chapter Eleven

Princess Eex Learns More

Meanwhile, back at the Brown Palace in the City of Lardiz, Princess Eex continued to work on her sums on the clean, gleaming parchments. She had heard the comment made by the elderly butler earlier, when he had said, 'I remember money, we used to use it and it made working much more enjoyable!'

The Princess wanted to know more about money and how it worked. She asked, 'Butler, please tell me how money used to be used on Zadril?'

The butler and the children sat on the brown, stone floor. The Lizard butler laid clean, gleaming parchment in front of him and started to speak as the children eagerly waited for the story to begin.

This is what the butler said: 'Well, it was very, very many sun-ups and moon-downs ago when we worked with money here on Zadril. The people were happy and they could earn as much money as they needed to buy the things they wanted to buy.

'The government saw that things were going very well, and that the people were prosperous and had a good life. However, the government wanted to become even richer than it was, so it decided that the people of Zadril should work for the government and not get paid for any of the work they did.

'The people behaved as they were told to for a while. But it wasn't long before they refused to go on working, and from that time on, the people of Zadril have not worked at all.

'The government was no longer a government that cared about the people, or the King and Queen. The government became wicked and tried to make people work. If they didn't work they were punished. But, even when they were punished, the people still refused to work if they were not paid for the work they did.

'Eventually, the government lost its power, but so did the people. The people didn't care about Zadril any more, or how they lived. They didn't care about how dirty Zadril had become. They didn't care about the buildings, parks and countryside. The parents didn't care about their children. Parents didn't care if their children went to school or not. The schools eventually closed down. The children no longer showed respect and nobody cared about anything any more. The farmers all stopped farming, so the only stuff to eat was junk food that the machines produced while they still went on running; we lost all quality in our lives!' he sighed.

'This is how it is now.'

Princess Eex noticed the sad look on the old Lizard butler's face as he spoke and remembered how life used to be. Princess Eex and Little Brother found the story interesting and begged the butler to tell them more. The butler had other ideas on his mind. He thought, 'I want to show the children how money works and the benefit of rewarding people for their effort and the good work they have done!'

He unrolled a large piece of parchment and started to draw and write. Both of the children joined him, writing with their writing sticks. They, too, were following the drawings the Zadrilian butler was creating. The children were not aware that he could do these things. Princess Eex looked at the butler and pulled on the sleeve of his tunic, then said, 'You never told us you knew all this!'

He winked his old eye at her as he continued to draw coins and to write about them. Princess Eex now knew some of the drawings and had learnt about money from Ziob. However, Princess Eex's Little Brother looked at the butler and wanted to know what he was doing. The young boy said, 'Mr Butler, why are you doing those drawings?'

The elderly butler said, 'I'm going to show you how money works, and tell you about the times when Zadril was a very good place to live.'

Princess Eex was now excited and said to her Little Brother, 'Look over there, on the parchments, can you see the money, the parts and shapes?' She continues, 'I learnt about those this sun-up time!'

The Lizard butler was deep in his thoughts and his drawings, but suddenly said to the surprised Princess, 'How did you learn about such things this sun-up, Princess Eex?' But he didn't wait for the Princess to answer his question: he seemed to forget straight away that he had asked her a question at all! He was thinking deeply about his own work as he sat on the brown stone floor of the Queen's apartment.

Taking a break from drawing, he explained, 'This is the value of money and how it works.' He was now drawing and speaking at the same time. The children looked on as the large piece of parchment became covered in drawings of coins. Little Brother had never seen anything like this before and wanted to know more and more. He asked, 'What do you do with those things?'

The butler said, 'I will show you a little later.'

The Lizard butler's parchments looked like this, covered in coins and writing. He explained the coins to the children as they watched him work.

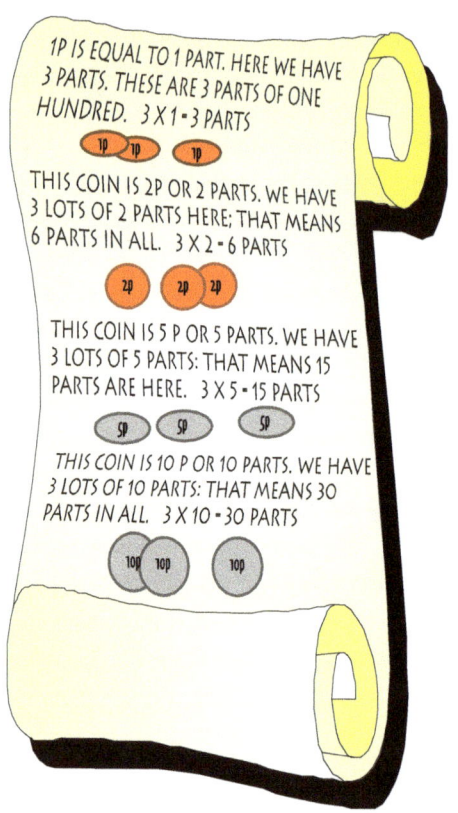

The Zadrilian butler continued explaining,

Princess Eex's Little Brother scratched his head and said, 'I don't understand all of this; it's too hard for me.'

The elderly butler had heard this before and knew how to answer the Little Brother. He replied, 'I will show you how these coins work and then you will see how interesting it all can be.' The butler unrolled another piece of parchment and laid it out on the brown stone floor and started to draw again. This time he drew different things. He asked Little Brother, 'Do you know what this is?' Princess Eex had seen this before and said, 'I think it's a ball!' The butler said, 'That's right.

'Now because the City of Lardiz was so run-down, and because the people didn't want to do anything or buy anything, all of the shops closed down, and then people couldn't buy anything even if they had wanted to!

'The toyshops of Lardiz closed down many generations ago. The Lizard children didn't know anything about toys or games, so they didn't know how to play!' The elderly butler thought out loud and said, forgetting his place, 'Why should the children know about toys? They have forgotten how to play anyway!' Princess Eex's Little Brother had never seen a ball before. He also, like the other Lizard children, had never played a game or played with friends.

The Lizard butler then said, 'The children used to play ball many, many generations ago but now they don't do much of anything!' He then thought and said quietly, 'It's very, very sad!' He continued, 'Now if you could buy a ball, would you?'

Both of the children answered quickly, 'Yes, yes!'

The Zadrilian butler then said, 'Let's see how many coins you have to spend to buy the ball.' He continued writing and drawing on the white parchment.

Princess Eex started to see now how money could work. She said excitedly, 'Do another.'

The butler unrolled another piece of clean and gleaming parchment and started to draw and write again. As he drew, he said, 'This is a drum and children used to play drums, but they don't do things like that now!'

Princess Eex heard his voice crackle and quiver; she looked at him and thought, 'I think he is going to cry!' The Princess looked at the old Lizard butler again and he, again, looked very sad, she thought.

He composed himself and then continued, 'Just suppose you want to buy the drum from your friend. Your friend says, "It will cost you 50 P." You have 60 P in your pocket; this is how your money will work.'

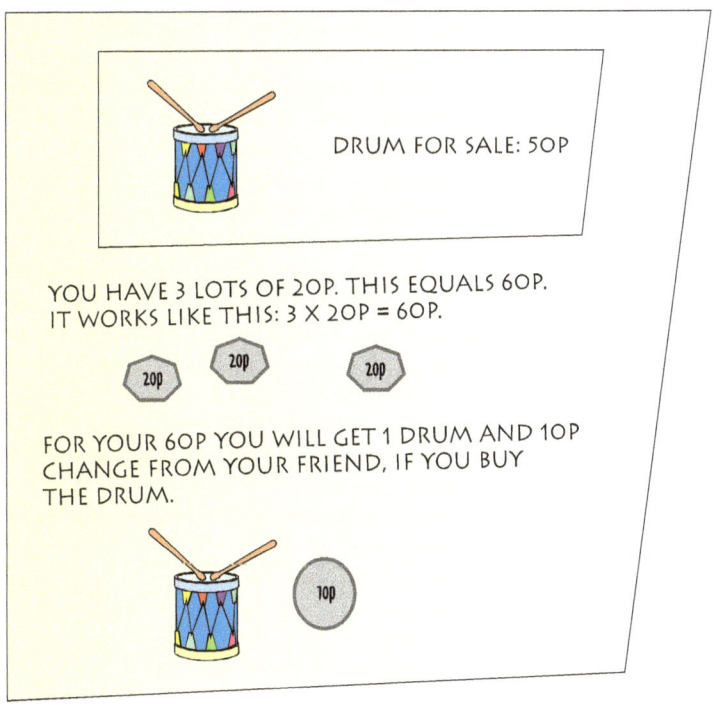

DRUM FOR SALE: 50P

YOU HAVE 3 LOTS OF 20P. THIS EQUALS 60P.
IT WORKS LIKE THIS: 3 X 20P = 60P.

FOR YOUR 60P YOU WILL GET 1 DRUM AND 10P CHANGE FROM YOUR FRIEND, IF YOU BUY THE DRUM.

Princess Eex said, 'Let's do one more.'

The elderly Lizard butler unrolled another parchment as he worked. He could see how interested the children were in what he was showing them, and was eager to keep the lesson going. Besides, he really enjoyed remembering how good Zadril used to be, he thought quietly to himself. He said, 'Just think of how hungry you get and how you would like to eat your favourite food.'

The butler then asked, 'Little Brother, what is your favourite food?'

Little Brother excitedly replied, 'Icen cones!'

'Good,' said the butler.

The butler continued with his ideas and asked, 'How much would you pay if you could buy an icen cone right now?'

Princess Eex's Little Brother didn't need to think for long. He knew he loved to eat icen cones with coloured sweets on the top and, as he thought of icen cones, Little Brother felt his mouth start to water. He had only eaten an icen cone once. He had enjoyed it so much and would dream of it, and hoped one day he would be able to eat cones again and again and again! As he thought about the icen cone, he said loudly, 'All the shapes I have!' The elderly butler now turned to Princess Eex. 'How much would you pay, Your Highness?'

Princess Eex, who had not really enjoyed the cone she had been given, pulled a face. '10 parts ... I suppose,' she said.

'So,' said the butler, 'an icen cone is worth 10 parts to you, but it's worth many shapes to you, Your Highness,' turning back to her brother.

'All the shapes I have!' cried Little Brother again. He stopped suddenly and then said sadly, 'But I don't have any shapes or parts, so I can't buy an icen cone!'

The elderly butler looked at Little Brother and then drew him an icen cone. The butler eagerly worked on the parchment, talking all of the time to the children.

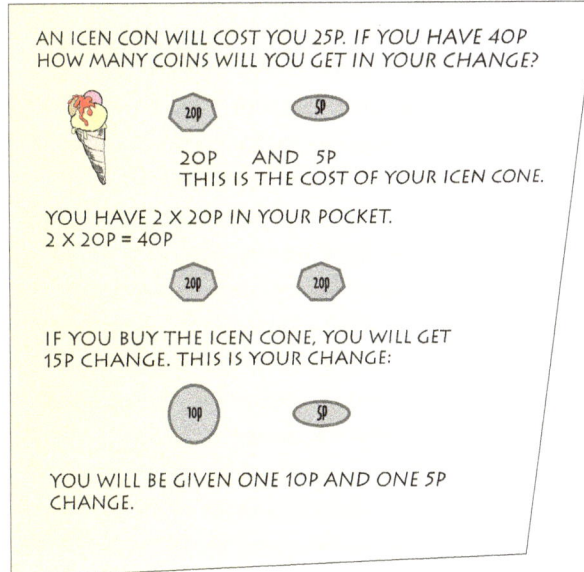

AN ICEN CON WILL COST YOU 25P. IF YOU HAVE 40P HOW MANY COINS WILL YOU GET IN YOUR CHANGE?

20P   AND   5P
THIS IS THE COST OF YOUR ICEN CONE.

YOU HAVE 2 X 20P IN YOUR POCKET.
2 X 20P = 40P

IF YOU BUY THE ICEN CONE, YOU WILL GET 15P CHANGE. THIS IS YOUR CHANGE:

YOU WILL BE GIVEN ONE 10P AND ONE 5P CHANGE.

'Do you see?' asked the butler. 'The cone costs more than you'd be happy to pay, my Royal Lady, so it's not very good value to you. However it costs much less than you would be prepared to pay, Your Highness,' turning to Little Brother, 'so you might think it was a real bargain at 25p!'

The elderly butler said, 'That is not all you can do with money; you can divide it.' He excitedly talks to the children, 'You divide money like this.'

He continued and asked the children, 'Do you remember when we had a visitor from the Planet Majania and he brought you some sweet honey drops? Do you remember how delicious they were?'

JUST THINK, IF THE SWEET HONEY DROPS WERE 15P EACH HOW MANY WOULD YOU GET FOR 90P?

20p 50p 10p 10p

THE SUMS WOULD WORK LIKE THIS:
20 + 50 + 10 + 10 = 90P

IF WE DIVIDE 15P INTO 90P WE WILL GET 6 SWEET HONEY DROPS!
90 ÷ 15 = 6

Princess Eex's Little Brother was scratching his head again as he stared at this sum. He said, 'I don't understand how you do that!'

Suddenly, the large door of the Brown Palace opened and Queen Irdzla entered with Will.

The elderly Lizard butler tried, in a hurry, to collect all the parchments up from the brown stone floor. He stumbled as he tried to bend down quickly, but there were too many parchments for him to pick up in one go! The butler thought to himself with exasperation and frustration, 'There are hundreds and hundreds of parchments that the children have been working on, and I simply cannot pick them all up quickly enough. Oh my goodness, what will happen next?'

The butler did not know what his fate would be! He stood waiting for the Queen to pass judgement on him. He had not asked permission to go to the dungeons with Princess Eex, nor had he asked permission to teach the children about shapes and parts, and how money works.

Chapter Twelve

What A Surprise!

Will was standing by Queen Irdzla's side watching what was going on, and could not help noticing the beautiful white paper the children and the butler had been working on. He thought quietly, 'The paper is magnificent; I have never seen anything so fine to write on!' Will looked around the Queen's apartment and realised that not a spot of brown stone floor could be seen.

The Queen was now standing in the middle of the large room next to Princess Eex; she looked down at the work and the parchments lying all over the floor. The elderly butler did not know what would happen next. He waited and thought, 'I haven't even asked permission to do this work with the children!'

The Queen knelt down on the floor and looked at every sheet of paper. She studied everyone, one after the other and looked at her children. She then looked at the elderly Lizard butler, smiled and clapped her hands. She held her arms out and both children ran to her. Queen Irdzla cried and said 'You know the secrets of our city now. We must teach all the children and their parents how to work with the money of Zadril again.'

Will stood in the doorway watching the children and the Queen. He then walked over and looked at the children's work and thought to himself, 'This is very good, to say the least!' Will thought he, too, could feel a lump developing in his throat.

He looked at the coins drawn on the crisp, clean parchments and then suddenly remembered his pay from the farmer on Ozimoth. He put his hand into his jeans' pocket and pulled out the pay packet, then looked at the writing on the envelope. It read:

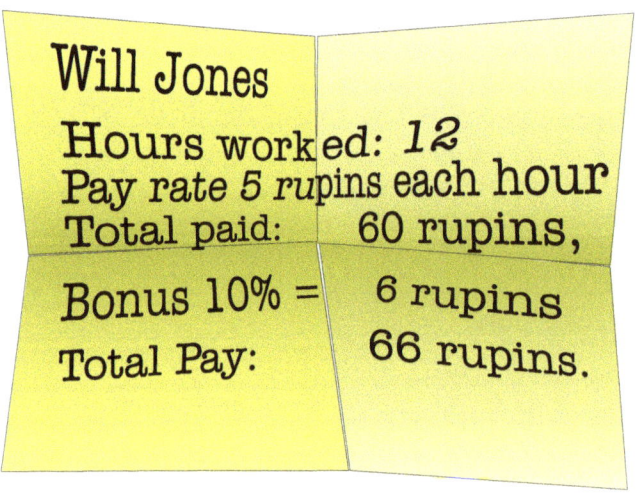

Will Jones
Hours worked: *12*
Pay rate 5 rupins each hour
Total paid: 60 rupins,
Bonus 10% = 6 rupins
Total Pay: 66 rupins.

Princess Eex saw Will looking at his 'payment for work' envelope from the Ozimoth farmer and came over to speak to him. She asked, 'What's that, Will?'

Will replied, 'This is the money I am paid when I work for the farmer on Ozimoth.' As he replied to Princess Eex, he opened the envelope and out fell some coins; they landed on the brown stone floor.

'Ping, ping, clamour, clamour' they went. The sound of the metal coins hitting the stone made the Lizard Queen and the butler stop instantly. The butler said loudly, 'My, it's many generations since I've heard that sound!'

The Queen too, agreed and replied, 'I have memories of hearing coins fall on stone floors but I have not heard that sound since I was a very small child.'

Princess Eex and Little Brother ran and picked up the fallen coins from the floor. Princess Eex said, as she gave them to Will, 'These look like the shapes and parts you were drawing on the parchment, Butler.'

The Queen and the Lizard butler laughed together as they too examined the coins from Ozimoth.

Will wanted to show the Zadrilian family how he worked with his money, so he emptied the pay packet out onto the brown stone floor. He sat down and said, 'Please join me. I want to show you how we work with our money on Ozimoth.' There were now five people sitting in a circle on the floor of the Queen's apartment.

Will counted out sixty-six rupins. Some of the rupins were in note currency and some in coin currency. Will said to the Zadrilians as they sat watching him, 'There are 100 pennies or 'P's to a rupin.' He took the money from the envelope and said, 'I have four money notes here;

each one is worth 10 rupins; that makes these four notes come to 40 rupins.' He asked the group, 'Do you agree?' The Queen said excitedly, 'Yes, that is just how we used to do it, wasn't it, Butler?'

The butler nodded his head and replied, 'Yes, Your Majesty, that is exactly how we did it!'

Will then took from the envelope four 5-rupin notes, and said, 'These four notes are worth 5 rupins each.'

He explained, 'So there are four larger notes that are worth 10 rupins each, and four smaller notes that are worth 5 rupins each. If I add these notes together:

      4 x 10-rupin notes = 40.00 rupins
and   4 x 5-rupin notes = 20.00 rupins.
This gives me 60 rupins altogether!'

'Yes, yes,' said the Lizard Queen as she clapped her hands in the air with excitement, 'that's exactly right!'

Will then shook the coins from the pay envelope and they landed on the stone floor of the Brown Palace. This is how the Ozimoth money looked.

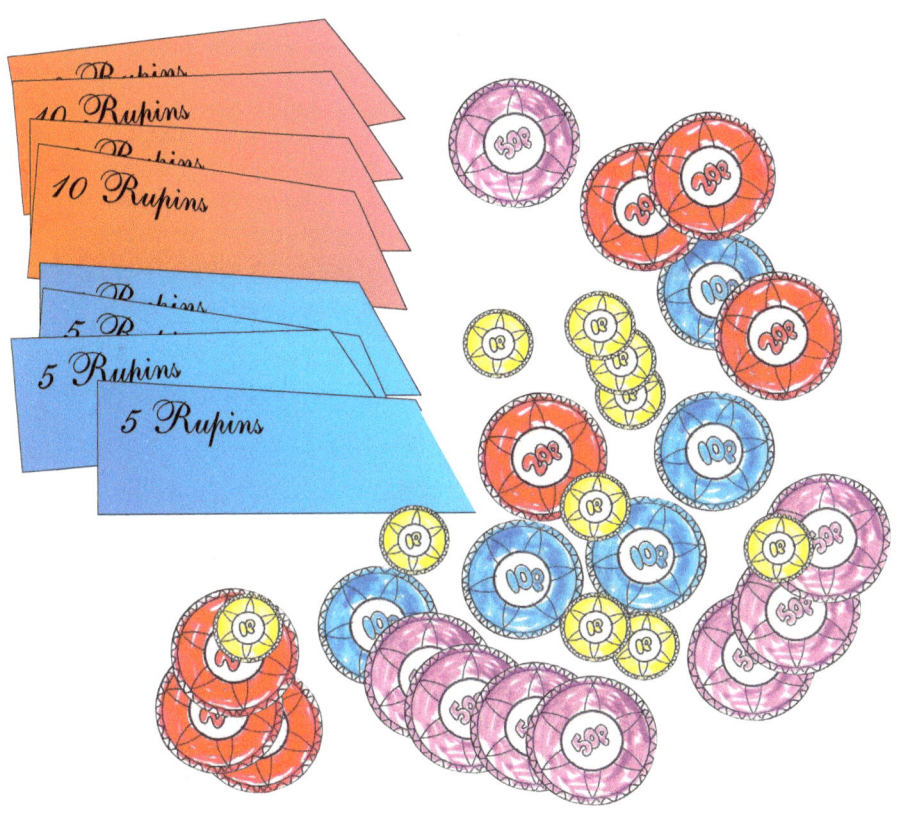

Will continued talking to the Zadrilians as they sat watching and listening to his story. Little Brother rubbed his sleepy eyes and said, 'I don't understand!' Will then thought 'I will have to make this more interesting for Little Brother's sake!'

He said, 'Little Brother, can you see the different colours and the different shapes of the coins?'

As he worked with the money he said, 'I have

4 x 10 rupins; that equals	R 40.00
4 x 5 rupins; that equals	R 20.00
8 x 50 pennies; that equals	R 4.00
7 x 20 pennies; that equals	R 1.40
5 x 10 pennies; that equals	R 0.50 and
10x 1 penny; that equals	<u>R 0.10</u>.
The total is	66.00 rupins

Will continued to explain how he works with his money. 'Here I have 66 rupins. I will now divide them into four piles.

'The first pile is my Special Money. I put 70% into this pile or seven-tenths.' Will took a deep breath and continued, 'It's easy to find out how to divide my money into tenths. I simply divide the whole amount by ten. Just like this. Here I have 66 rupins and if I divide 66 by 10 I get 6.60. This is my sum: R66 ÷ 10 = 6.60 rupins. Then I multiply 6.60 by 7: this gives me 70% or seven-tenths.' Will continued, 'My Special Money is always 70%. If I multiply 6.60 by 7 I get the sum of R46.20P.

'I now have 19 rupins and 80 pennies left. If I divide 19 rupins and 80 pennies by 3, this is my sum: R19.80P ÷ 3. I find that comes to 6 rupins and 60 pennies. I then put R6.60 into three separate piles of money. My money now looks like this.'

Will explains, 'Pile 1 has 70% of the money I earned, which is R46.20P.

Special Money Rupins   7/10

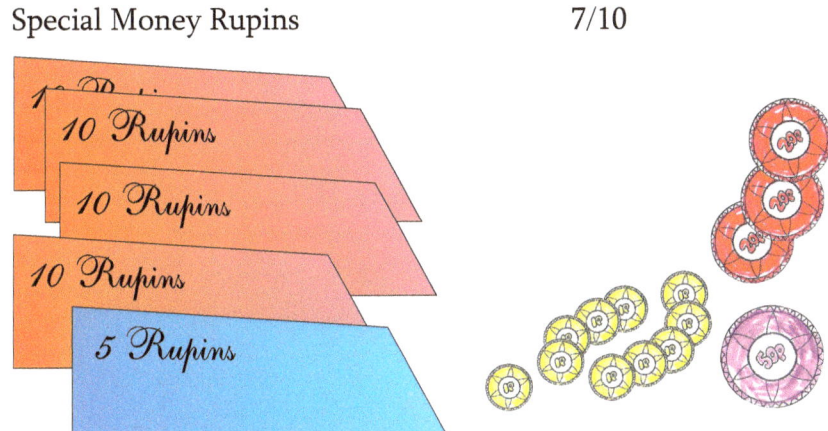

Rupipns   R46.20 pennies

'In Pile 2, I give 10% to the children's home, that is R6.60P.

Money for the children in the   1/10
Children's Home

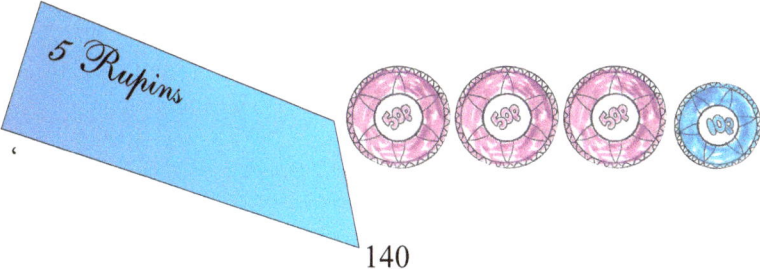

Rupins: R6.60 pennies

'Pile 3, I also put 10% in, and this is my secret money. Will continued speaking to the group while they sat on the stone floor of the Brown Palace of Lardiz.

'This is my Secret Money,' explains Will.

Secret Money   1/10

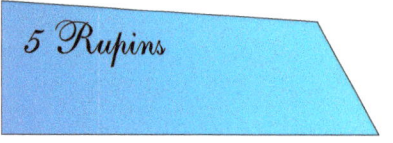

Rupins   R6.60 pennies

Will explains, 'I keep this money for my personal projects and the things I want to do in the future. I also collect stamps and coins from other planets. I can buy them with my secret money.' He hesitates a little and says, 'I don't often tell people about my secret money!

'I sometimes, sell the stamps and coins I've collected and paid for with my secret money. I will only sell the stamps and coins at a profit. When they are sold, I put the extra money I've made back into my secret money!'

Queen Irdzla was listening with interest to Will's words and nodded her head. She then said, 'Will, I like that idea: it is your capital and your investment.' Will looked at the

Queen and replied, 'Yes, Your Majesty, that is exactly what it is!'

Will now pointed in the direction of his savings money. 'Pile 4 is my savings money. I also put 10% into this pile.'

Savings Money   1/10

Rupins   R6.60 pennies

Will explains to the group, 'With my savings money I put it into the bank or building society and try never to spend it. One day I will move it into an investment that is larger and that I understand.'

Little Brother then burst into a shout and said, 'I know, I know, you have Special Money, Money for the Children's Home, your Secret Money and your Savings Money. Yes, I understand!' Queen Irdzla was surprised, and gave Little Brother a kiss on his cheek, as she felt excited too!

The Lizard Queen then showed interest in Will's Special Money and said to him, 'Will, what is your Special Money for?'

Will promptly replied, 'I am now in high school and I need things for school, so I buy those things; but I also use that money to buy the things I need.' He continues, 'It helps my mum and dad. They don't have to buy everything I need. Also, sometimes I go to the movies with my friend Ben!' He suddenly remembered Ben and that they were supposed to be going to see the latest 007 movie – 'Ben loves James Bond films!' Will recalled. As Will finished thinking, he was suddenly brought back to Planet Zadril and being in the Brown Palace.

Suddenly, the rooms of the palace once again filled with laughter and, as this was all happening, the Lizard Queen, the butler and the children started to change. They no longer resembled lizards. Their skin changed from greenish and scaly to a light, smooth golden-brown colour.

They looked at each other and realised that the way of thinking and the way they had been living in destitution was now lifting from their lives. They knew now that things were changing very quickly!

The elderly butler went and quietly sat in his brown stone chair. He thought silently, 'We are now back to the people we were, "the people of our ancestors" !' As he sat, he thought, 'The people of Lardiz are now ready to learn.'

Queen Irdzla called the people together and told them, 'We will form a new government that will be elected by everybody. We will do this instantly so that our children can now be educated, and the people of Lardiz can start to earn money again and enjoy their lives.'

The people started to cheer and they too began to lose their lizard appearance. They then started to clean their city and to remove the rubbish that had been littering the streets of Lardiz for generations. They started to clean and remove the dirt and grime and dust from the city buildings and, as they did, a city of crystal-clear stone appeared!

Will saw now the true people of Lardiz. They were proud and happy. They were eager to work and to learn, and it was as though the people of the city had returned from many, many generations ago, he thought.

Will was now ready to leave the Planet Zadril. He suddenly recalled, 'Oh no, I have a long journey in a worn-out and run-down spaceship!' He was secretly hoping he would land safely back on the Planet of Grigan!

Chapter Thirteen

The Journey To Ozimoth

It was a bumpy journey back to the Planet Grigan. The old spaceship managed to fly into the very narrow cave mouth, leading deep down into the centre of Grigan to the City of Epahs. Will said his goodbyes to the people of Zadril and to Princess Eex, who had travelled with him. As he was leaving the ship, the Princess put a small piece of parchment into his hand. She told him, 'You are not to look at this until you're back on Ozimoth.'

He accepted her gift and put it into his jeans' pocket. Then he picked her up and gave her a great big hug and said, 'I hope we meet again, Princess Eex.' He then put her gently back down onto the ground of the Planet Grigan. He suddenly remembered to ask, 'Oh, Princess Eex, what is your brother's name?'

She replied, 'Rufute. It's too difficult to say all of the time, so I just call him Little Brother.'

Will thought, 'Yes, that is a bit too difficult to say all of the time!'

He made his way back through the rocky cave and to the Hall of Learning of the City of Epahs. There, Ziob and Chet were waiting for him. Will did not know that Ziob had made a visit to Zadril while he was travelling to find the Zarwids. He tried to explain where he had been, and Ziob's answer was, 'You were on a journey, and we understand!'

She then said, 'We have learned much from your visit, Will. I must soon escort you up to the Grigan surface so that you can speak to the Grigan Leader and do the job he has brought you to this planet to do. But, before you return to the city of Jade, the Space Masters would like to speak to you.'

Ziob led Will to the innermost chamber in the Library of the City of Epahs. The Space Masters of the Planets were there, seated in a circle behind a large, round, green marble table. Will waited patiently for the Senior Master to speak.

The room was filled with deafening silence. Will quickly looked around at the number of Space Masters; he estimated that there were at least one hundred Masters in this one room! The Space Masters sat waiting and Will stood waiting. More Space Masters came into the room. Some of them didn't worry about using doors; they would simply appear and then disappear – as if coming and going through the thick walls of the room!

When all the Space Masters were present and had settled into their seats, the Senior Space Master spoke to Will and the other Masters. He said, 'The Grigan Leader has brought you to the Planet Grigan to speak to the children of Grigan and to us, The Space Masters.' He took a deep and long pause and then continued, while Will and the other Masters listened attentively. 'We know that you have visited the Planet Zadril and met the Zarwids.' He then asked Will. 'Did you learn anything from your trip to Zadril, Will?'

Will replied, 'Well, yes, I did. I learnt that most people want to learn how to live a good life. People like to work, and people like to be paid fairly for the work they do.'

The Senior Space Master nodded his head at Will's answer and then there were mutterings from all the other Space Masters in the innermost chamber. When the deafening silence came back over the room, the Senior Space Master asked Will another question. 'And what do you think work does for people, Will?'

Will replied, 'At school on Ozimoth we have been learning subjects like citizenship and friendship, and we have learnt that through treating people fairly people will have a good and positive self-esteem. Mr Wakeman, our teacher, has said, "If you have a good, positive self-esteem you can accomplish your dreams and achieve your life's wishes." '

The Senior Space Master looked for a while at Will. The other Space Masters nodded their heads in agreement with what they had just heard Will say.

Will then heard the Senior Space Master repeat his words, 'Positive self-esteem, achieve your life's wishes and accomplish your dreams!' Will continued, 'In fact, Mr Wakeman always says, "You should always feel good about who you are because there is only one of you and you are unique"!'

The Space Master seemed to grow taller and taller and his chest wider and wider as Will said these words. He then said, after thinking about Will's words, 'We have all learned a great deal from what you have told us about your teacher, Mr Wakeman.'

The Space Master stood up from his seat and said, 'Will, you must visit us again in the future but now you must go back to the surface of Grigan. You will find that, though time has passed on your journey, it has stood almost still up there.'

With these words of farewell, Will started to walk with Ziob from the innermost chamber of the Library. As they reached the large door, the Senior Space Master said, 'Will, there is one other point. Have you heard of the Planet of the Black Sun?'

Will and Ziob looked back at the Space Masters, who were waiting for his reply. Will replied, 'Yes.' The Senior Space Master nodded his head and looked at Will waiting for any other explanation that he might have. Will then shrugged his shoulders and replied, 'I have been told that the planet is a dark planet and to avoid going there!' Both Ziob and Will waited for the next question to come from the Senior Space Master, but he sat back down in his chair without saying a word. Will and Ziob then walked through the large door and into the centre of the Library and were surrounded by a bright, thick green light.

Will soon found he was spinning up and up and up, spiralling with Ziob up to the surface of the Planet Grigan. He landed on his feet under the shade of the large green tree in the centre of Jade in bright sunshine. Will realised, 'This is where I started my journey to Epahs and Zadril!' He looked around and, in the distance, he could see the Grigan Leader rushing towards him. The Leader said, after much panting and rushing, 'My, I'm glad to see you. Did you go and speak to some other person, or did you just go for a long walk?'

Will replied, 'A bit of both, I think!'

The Grigan Leader had no time for explanations; he had all of the children of Grigan ready to listen to Will in the big sporting arena. They were ready to listen to the story of Will Jones! As Will and the Leader rushed to the arena, the Leader said, 'Will, please hurry, there are many children and young adults, not to mention the King and Queen of Grigan, waiting to hear you speak!'

Will entered the arena and there before him were thousands and thousands of children and young people waiting to hear about the adventures of the famous Will Jones! Starting to speak, he looked down to the front row and saw the seven Princes and Princesses of Grigan and, sitting next to them, were the King and Queen. Will suddenly thought of Princess Eex; and said, 'This is a story about a little girl who wanted to learn. She wanted to learn about sums and about other people living on different planets. She wanted to learn everything that she could possibly learn.

On her planet, the children and their parents did not learn; they didn't go to school; there weren't any schools. The parents were not taught, nor were their grandparents taught. For generations they were a miserable race. Their planet was dirty and there was rubbish in the streets. The people didn't worry about how their city looked. There was deep dirt and dust over everything. The children were hungry and so were their parents, but they had no heart to do anything for themselves. The people were dying because they had forgotten how to live.

'One little girl had a mother who really cared about her children and wanted a better life for them. The mother was determined to find out the answers; she wanted to know why the people were acting the way they were, and how they could change their way of life for a better one.

'The mother found out the answer. She discovered that, when people work, they need to be rewarded. On this planet, the government stopped paying the people for the work they did. In the end the people decided not to work. Their city became very dirty and their children didn't go to school. The people were hungry and lazy, miserable, and did not enjoy anything in their lives.

'The mother decided that this was not going to be any good for the planet, the city, the people and their children, so she decided to make some changes.

'The mother is Queen Irdzla of Lardiz on the Planet Zadril. The little girl is Princess Eex. The Queen is making changes and the people are being paid for the work they now do. They have learned that being lazy does not help the planet or its citizens.

'The people of Lardiz have suffered and now they are determined not to live that way again.'

Will cleared his throat. 'There's one other thing I want to say. It's not part of the story I've just told, but it's part of the lesson that the Queen learned. Money can be divided into two separate piles when it is given to you. The two piles are gift money and earned money.

'Remember, to be paid money for the work you do shows you that somebody else values your time and effort in doing a job. The payment is because you have 'earned' that money.

'When you are given money because somebody loves you and respects you that is "gift" money.'

The Grigan Leader listened carefully to every word that Will said to the children of Grigan. When Will had finished speaking, the Grigan Leader ran to Will and picked him up in his familiar way – almost crushing his ribs – and then kissed him on the cheek. Will was very embarrassed at this. The King and Queen, their seven children and the other children of Grigan stood, clapped their hands and cheered as they saw the action of the Leader.

It was long after sundown when Will finished his talk to the children and it was now time to go back to Ozimoth. The Grigan Leader put his great lumpy, bumpy arm around Will's shoulder as they walked through the very clean and green city of Jade. The Leader said, 'My young friend, I think we will see a change in the children of Grigan now.' He then continued, 'Was that a real story you have just told to the children of Grigan?' Will looked at the Grigan Leader and smiled!

Soon Will, the Leader and the Grigan guards were aboard the very fast spaceship and speeding towards Ozimoth. 'The spaceship has reached hyper-sonic speed through space and is travelling faster than the speed of light!' thought Will. He looked out at the planets as the ship passed them. In the distance he could see the Planets of Spectron and Majania. He knew that, on this journey, he would not visit them but, he thought, 'perhaps I will in the future!'

At last they were approaching home. Deep down from outer space they flew. Through the clouds he could just make out the island of Ozimoth. It was so beautiful it took his breath away, and he knew now how lucky he was to live on such a healthy island and planet. The ship landed at the end of Will's street. He now realised that he had forgotten about his bike and how the wheel had been buckled in the accident! However, the Grigan Leader had not forgotten. An inside spaceship door slid open and a Grigan soldier was standing with the repaired bike, waiting for Will.

Will looked at the Grigan Leader and knew that, in the Leader, he had a very good space friend. The Leader said, 'Will, until we meet you again.' He gave Will another huge hug as the boy left the spaceship.

Will took his bike and ran down the ship's ramp into the damp autumn air of home.

He stood and watched the spaceship's door as it slid closed. Suddenly, in the blink of an eye, the spaceship was gone from sight. Will felt inside his jeans' pocket for his mobile phone to ring Ben. He remembered, 'my phone is at home!'

At home, the first thing Will did was ring Ben on his mobile. Ben replied, 'Hi Will! Will you be over later? Don't forget, we are going to the party or maybe the movies later. I really want to see that new 007 movie!'

Will replied, 'No, I won't forget. I'll see you, then.' As he went to put the mobile phone back into his jeans' pocket he felt a small piece of parchment rub against his fingers. He brought the brilliant white parchment out of his pocket, unfolded it and there, written in very neat writing, was a message; it said this.

TO MY FRIEND WILL
FROM PRINCESS EEX
ON THE PLANET OF ZADRIL

A little time later, Will was on his way to meet Ben when something began bothering him. He felt strangely uncomfortable but didn't know why. He was riding his newly repaired bike and kept thinking, 'Why do I keep thinking about the Planet of the Black Sun? I know I will never go there, so why should it bother me?'

[Find out in the next book in *Will Jones' Space Adventures: The Children of the Black Sun* – chilling!]

Other Books by Christine Thompson-Wells:

Will Jones' Space Adventures & The Money Formula
This is the first children's book in the Will Jones series that is written on cash flow and money management. To capture the child's imagination the series takes the child to many distant planets where other people live, work and manage their money. On Will's first adventure, through showing the King of the Planet Spectron and the Leader from the Planet Grigan how to control their money, a major war is avoided. The people of the planets learn that through dialogue they have the capability to work together.

www.ingramcontent.com/pod-product-compliance
Lightning Source LLC
Chambersburg PA
CBHW062059290426
44110CB00022B/2647